The Shining Within Me
Communications from the Afterlife

By Freddie Rivera

Printed in the United States of America

First Printing, 2014

ISBN-13: 978-1499358889
ISBN-10: 1499358881

Printed by Createspace

http://www.mediumfreddierivera.com

Dedication

This book is dedicated to my mother, Mercedes Rivera. Without her, I might have never known what unconditional love really is. Her dedication to her children and her fight to keep us all together is unparalleled. Te adoro, mami, con todo mí corazón y mí alma (I adore you, Mom, with all of my heart and soul).

The Shining Within Me

Contents

ACKNOWLEDGMENTS

The Shining Within Me is the result of the contributions of hundreds of people who have allowed me to come into their lives by way of mediumship. One of those people, in particular, is Medea Yorba. I truly believe that the other side sends us living angels, and Medea is just that. Without her coming into my life, this book would still be waiting on my computer collecting dust. Medea did most of the editing and worked hard to see that *The Shining Within Me* was finished and, at last, here it is. I can't begin to express how appreciative I am to her. She is one of the most selfless and giving people I have ever met. Medea, we are friends forever, and I love you.

I would also like to thank those listed below for allowing me to use their testimonials and stories. All of you will be part of my life forever.

Patricia Seward-Lazaro, Simone Gabbay, Clytie Koehler, Josie Varga, Medea Yorba, Kathleen Theresa Ferber Eggert, Billie Layland, Kalila Smith, Angie Pechak Printup, Trina Trimm King, Lee Van Zyl, and Ann Marie Martin.

When I was thinking of who I should ask to write a foreword for me, the very first person who came into my mind was the renowned psychic medium Concetta Bertoldi. I prayed that she would say yes; as always, my prayers were answered. Thank you, Concetta!

Foreword

A fascinating read, this book depicts the trials and tribulations of a traumatic childhood, full of frightening and misunderstood encounters with the paranormal. It offers a clear picture of how Freddie's psychic and mediumistic abilities emerged, amid a meager and humble life in Spanish Harlem, and how he uses those abilities today to help others.

Concetta Bertoldi

Introduction

I feel that the essence of spiritual practice is your attitude toward others. When you have a pure, sincere motivation, then you have right attitude toward others based on kindness, compassion, love and respect. ~ Dalai Lama

In early 2009, I was geared up to write a book because everyone else was doing it. I didn't have much experience as a psychic medium yet; the book was intended to be an autobiography of myself—how boring. Mind you, I am not a professional writer; most people who put out books are not. That is why there are editors and proofreaders. Thank God for that!

In any event, I ended up with 15 chapters by mid-2011. Now what? I shared some of my chapters with friends, and as poorly written as those chapters were, they liked them. Some were surprised at the content. Surprise, I am a psychic medium! Well, it was a surprise to those who didn't already know it.

As the years went by, my chapters collected dust on my computer's hard drive. I did not yet know what to do with them, but I had backed them up in case my hard drive crashed. I feel that this book was meant to happen, but I wasn't ready. I felt that my Spirit Guides and Angels were holding me back—stopping me because publication would have been a mistake with the content as it was then. I didn't have an important message to give the world yet.

Through the years, I gave mediumship readings, but there were some that stood out; those were the ones that the other side was waiting for. The book gradually took shape. It includes glimpses of my personal life that highlight some of the hard lessons I have learned in this lifetime so far. My life isn't over yet; the lessons will keep coming.

My Spirit Guides and Angels don't impose anything on me; they do not infringe on my free will. But they do make suggestions. I felt that this book should be a testament as to how powerful a mediumship reading can be, and the positive results that often follow. It's a method of healing. The more powerful the evidence that the consciousness survives after the physical body has died, the more powerful the healing's potential.

I believe this book is important. In it, I share my early struggles with gifts I didn't understand. Other important chapters will help validate the impact a mediumistic reading can bring. *A Life-Saving Reading, Giving Back – Voice of Our Angels*, and *Proof Positive* make clear what the readings really are all about – closure and healing.

You will read how my spiritualism cleared my life up. I have learned how much I am loved by those heavenly beings I describe in this book; we all are. They don't wave a magic wand and make everything negative in our lives go away; we have to be active participants in healing ourselves. But when we listen, they aid us.

As in every case, God gave all of us the gift to heal ourselves and to heal others. There are probably as many different approaches to these gifts as there are individuals in the world. My methods have evolved within the unique experiences and circumstances of my life.

Chapter One

1963 – The Beginning

"I believe in intuitions and inspirations. I
sometimes *feel* that I am right. I do not
know that I am." - *Albert Einstein*

"I have a dream that one day this nation will rise up and live
out the true meaning of its creed: We hold these truths to be
self-evident; that all men are created equal." Dr. Martin
Luther King, *I Have a Dream,* August 28th, 1963.

This first chapter is called *1963 — The Beginning* because, for
me, 1963 was the year when it all began.

I remember the very day; it was a beautiful sunny summer
day. I was six years old. All of us, my mom, my brothers and
sisters and I, were gathered in our tiny living room, eyes glued
to our small black and white TV. The typically very poor
reception could not discourage us from avidly watching Dr.
Martin Luther King's speech: *I Have a Dream.*

As young as I was, I was very aware of the tense and serious
conversation that went on among the adults during this time.
I heard it everywhere we went. Then, and in the years
following, I was very aware of the discussions that always
revolved around the same two issues: equal rights among the
races and the war in Vietnam. There seemed to be a constant
and continuous debate going on. As a young child, I grew
tired of hearing about it. It seemed that everyone had an
opinion, and *everyone* felt it *needed* to be heard. Me? All I

wanted to do was play, and eat my mother's wonderful Puerto Rican cooking.

We frequently heard that someone else in our neighborhood had lost a son in the war. Television coverage was constantly focused on the war protestors or the racial riots. There was a lot of discussion about young men within our community (and everywhere else) who wanted to escape the mandatory draft. There were those who were running away up north to Canada, before "their number came up." And, when a number *did* come up, the buzz ran through the neighborhood quickly about whose son would be shipping out next.

In our household, however, we thought we were fortunate that we were all too young to be drafted. My mother was very relieved about that, and hoped the war would be over before any of us reached that age. It *was* over by then. Even later in life when I joined the Army, it was during a time of relative peace. But at that time, there was no indication that I was soon to be embroiled in a different kind of struggle.

While those complex issues dominated the social and political debate, I was only vaguely conscious of them. On that historical day, August 28, 1963, with my humble family huddled around that little old TV set, I was focused on other events that were happening specifically to me. We still lived in apartment number 31, and to this day, I feel that apartment was a passageway for spiritual entities.

But I am jumping ahead of myself. I want to share with you a little of my background: In early 1953, several years before I was born, my brother Miguel Jr., who was one year old, was "kidnapped." My father told my mother that he was taking their child to visit some of his family in another town. Mom agreed, but after a couple of days had passed with no word from him, she became concerned. My brother had not been returned to her, and there was no word from my father. Finally she learned from one of my father's cousins that Miguel Senior had actually taken their son out of Puerto Rico to New York City.

My mom, Mercedes, was beside herself with worry; she didn't know what to do. Several days went by before she received a letter from my father telling her that he would not be returning to Puerto Rico. If she wanted to be with him and their son, she would have to join them in New York.

My parents had no formal education and didn't have much money. Their life in Puerto Rico had been a meager one. Beyond the fact that my mother was desperate to hold her baby in her arms again, she saw the move as an opportunity to advance in the world. She wrote back that she would come.

Mom had never been to any other place in the world, or even on an airplane. She was filled with a mixture of excitement and sadness. She understood that an adventure was before her, but she also knew she was leaving her beloved family behind. It was especially hard for her to leave my grandmother, Jovíta, whom she loved dearly.

In 1951, when my parents had first met my mother was already a widow with two children — Miriam, who was nine years old, and Benjamin, who was seven. While they waited for my father to send their tickets, my mother began to prepare them for the reality that they were leaving Puerto Rico behind. As soon as he could, my father sent the tickets, but there were only two. One was for my mother and one for my sister Miriam, but none for Benjamin. My father had decided that my brother was not coming to New York. He would be just one more mouth to feed, an unwanted extra expense.

My mother insisted that she wasn't going to leave Benjamin in Puerto Rico; if he wasn't coming, no one was coming. Soon after that, the third ticket arrived and the journey began. They didn't have much, so the trip was fairly easy. They didn't need passports to travel, since Puerto Ricans are American citizens and that helped to expedite the move.

And so, in March of 1953, my mom, my sister Miriam, and my brother Benjamin (nicknamed Pete) – all terrified and excited at the same time – landed in the big, daunting city of New York. They knew nothing about this new place and none of them spoke a word of English.

Their immediate destination turned out to be a small, over-crowded apartment that belonged to my father's parents. They shared a small, crowded room. I never knew those grandparents. My mother describes these as difficult days. My father's family certainly did not treat them very well, and this is a sore subject with my mother to this day.

It was six months before my father was able to borrow money to pay the first month's rent and a security deposit for an apartment. It was money that was hard to pay back, especially hard in those days, unless one had a good paying job.

Nevertheless, my family was grateful to move into that small, two-bedroom-and-one-bath apartment. It had a tiny kitchen and living space, and it was on the sixth floor. The building, number 124, was on 107th street between Lexington and Park in Manhattan. The tenement was old and had no elevator. The neighborhood was called Spanish Harlem, also known as *El Barrio*. It began on East 96th Street and ended at 120th Street in Manhattan, just short of where Black Harlem began.

I will never forget that place; so much transpired for me there. I was born in 1957 at Mount Sinai hospital on Fifth Avenue. That hospital was very well known for treating many of the rich and famous. My mother tells me that, at nearly ten pounds, I was her most difficult delivery.

By the time of my birth, there were already seven people in that little apartment: my mother, father, Miriam, Benjamin, Miguel Jr., Abigail, and Augustine. It wasn't the greatest place to live, but it was all we had. We made the best of it. The building wasn't kept up very well; the superintendent always took weeks to get needed repairs done. We had a constant struggle to keep the roaches and mice under control.

I asked my mother one day: "Why did you name me Freddie?" She told me that my father had named me after his supervisor. He was working at the Empire State building as a cook's helper at the time, and he and his supervisor 'Freddie' were very good buddies. I never met the man, but I guess my father must have thought highly of him, to make me his namesake.

Making monthly grocery trips was exhausting — carrying grocery bags up six flights of stairs. We got our cardiovascular exercise, whether we wanted to or not. The building was old, and a bit creepy, with fire escapes that reminded me of scenes from *The West Side Story*. There are mostly multistory brick tenement buildings in Spanish Harlem, with a scattering of project housing all around. The tenement buildings were built around the early 1900s. At that time, fires were common. All tenements must be built with fire escapes mounted on the outside walls of the buildings.

I spent the first ten years of my life living in that sixth-floor apartment. We had the hallway and the areas outside of our building to play in. The rules were that we could not go anywhere beyond the perimeter of the building. We had to do our homework, of course, before we did anything else, such as play or watch TV. We played with our neighbor kids; the building was full of them.

The streets of New York City express the soul of its neighborhoods. They are the pathways to some of the world's most essential destinations. For generations, New Yorkers and visitors have strolled, shopped, and socialized on sidewalks and street corners. Pedestrian-friendly streets are the city's most fundamental asset.

When I was growing up in El Barrio, the streets were mostly dirty and neglected. This was largely because during that time the city government didn't care much for our neighborhood. There was a great deal of racism, and our community needs were not addressed. Police brutality was out of control.

My father, who was a severe alcoholic, crossed over when I was four years old. My mom told me that when he didn't have any money to buy liquor, he drank rubbing alcohol. He was an angry drunk, and my mom endured a lot of physical and mental abuse because of this. It was perhaps understandable that even his own family didn't love him.

They really didn't love him; he knew it. This was probably something he brought upon himself with his drinking, at least in part. I always thought that if they had loved him, they would have helped my mother with his children after he was gone.

I believe that my father was abused as a child, hence his low self-esteem. Apparently all of his life people put him down, treating him like he was insignificant. He was fortunate to have met my mother, but she, on the other hand, was not so lucky. The liquor and the malevolent attachments that I

6

believe instigated a lot of his behavior destroyed him. My mom is a survivor of it all.

I remember going to my father's funeral and, although I was only four years old, I remember clearly how the fragrance of the flower arrangements permeated the air. For many years after that, I hated the smell of flowers. They reminded me of the sense of death that surrounded me that day. Even so young, I was profoundly affected: I knew what death felt like. Today, I have traveled a long way from being that little boy, and I love the smell of flowers.

After my father crossed over, his family washed their hands of us all. Apparently they had shifted the malice they had for him onto us. I feel this nastiness had always existed, and we never saw or heard from any of them again, except for one aunt and her children. We played with those cousins; they lived in our building. Mom told me that even on holidays or special occasions, my father's family never acknowledged us as part of their own. They abandoned us and seemingly forgot about us.

My mother recently learned that Amada, one of my father's sisters, had crossed over. I have never felt her presence. I have wondered how she feels about her behavior toward us now that she has moved on. She may have to deal with the karma she inflicted on herself while she was here. If she ever does come to me, I don't know how I will react. I guess I might ask her "why did you abandon us and transfer the animosity you felt for our father onto us?"

Considering her actions in this life and the feelings my family has about her, however, Amada probably won't come around now.

Trying to Make a Fresh Start

My mother was without the support of her family; they were far away in Puerto Rico. My father's death left my mother penniless, with six children to fend for by herself. She had no education and didn't speak a word of English.

A friend of hers, Juanita, who was a devout Pentecostal, showed up faithfully every Sunday to take us to church. We kids would hide under the bed to get out of going. Juanita took my mom to the welfare office, where she helped her fill out the application for assistance. The application was written only in English back then. To my mom's relief, we qualified for public assistance in addition to widow's compensation from the Social Security Administration. Mom took solace in the fact that she could pay the bills and feed her children. Her attitude changed and she was happier — less depressed. She vowed not to remarry or have anything to do with men ever again. To this day, at ninety-six, her determination has never wavered.

My mom is someone very special. She is very loving and caring, everything a mother should be, always. Every night before I go to bed, I thank God for her. We didn't have much, but we made do. After my father passed, we were generally happier; things were definitely better for us in some ways.

As a very spiritual person today, I have learned much about forgiveness. I know that we are born and reborn to learn lessons. Our experiences living a physical life on this earth plane may have been written before we reincarnated. Perhaps we have come here to correct errors we committed in a past life, to fulfill our karma. I feel that part of our lesson when we reincarnate is to absorb what we have missed in the previous

8

life. I do not know all of the answers, but I look forward to acquiring them.

I was so young at the time of my father's passing that I have no memory of him; everything I have ever heard about him is negative. I was too young to have seen or remembered any of the abuse. As an adult, I have had contact with him through other mediums. Twice my father has come through. The gist of the messages I was given was that he is proud of me; he is happy I found my calling as a medium, and he loves me. I cannot describe how good it was to receive those messages.

Those mediums didn't know a thing about me. They didn't know that my father had crossed over. They didn't even know that I was a medium. I had not given them any information concerning myself. True mediums don't want any information, just validation. They did give me validation that I confirmed was accurate. They also acknowledged that my father had crossed over due to his drinking.

I cannot do a mediumship reading for myself. I might imagine that a loved one is coming to me. I might feel, see, and hear what I want to because I miss and love them.

I usually go to several medium friends of mine for readings. You might say, we barter our readings for the same reasons I mentioned above: we are unable to do readings for ourselves. Don't get me wrong, we do feel our loved ones around us. We do feel the love they want to express to us. But for me, to have another medium bring through what the loved one wants to say is best.

There is a movie my niece Rosalinda likes; it's called *Mermaids*. I sat down and watched it with her one day. The movie starred Cher and Wynona Rider. Rider's character longs to meet her biological father. The only photo she has of him is one that only shows his shoes. *Well*, I thought, *at least my mother has one wrinkled black-and-white photo of my father.* He was posing up on the roof. This at least gives me some idea of what he looked like.

Sensing the Invisible

As a young child, I began to sense the history connected with our building: energies from an extensive past, ingrained into the walls, and bricks. There was suffering in that building. I was having psychic impressions that I did not understand and that frightened me at that time; one does not identify with psychic impressions if they are unknown to them. There was nothing in my experience thus far that would have prepared me for what was happening to me.

Thinking back as clearly as I can to what I felt then, I recall sensing that a few people had been hurt or maybe murdered in that building. I also felt joy from devoted and loving families. While I was experiencing these impressions, because of my lack of knowledge, I thought that I was making up stories in my head. This seems unlikely, though, because the images in my head just came to me without any purposeful thought on my part.

Like many old tenement buildings in the city, the building swarmed with the residuals of bad and good energies. At times, I would inadvertently touch a wall or door while playing in the hallway. Suddenly, I would start to see little movies — images in my mind's eye. These caused strong, unnerving feelings and impressions. They were *very* uncomfortable. I felt anger, frustration, and confusion. My psychic abilities were not yet known to me; I wouldn't have had any way to know what they meant, how to deal with them, or even to name them. The only option for a young child in those circumstances was to avoid thinking about

10

something so unsettling. I simply paid as little attention as possible to those impressions. I thought that I was imagining things.

Much later, when maturity and education allowed a better understanding, I learned that those impressions were caused by the residue of "intoxication." Today I know that when I touched the hallway walls, I would pick up on psychic impressions that were recorded within those walls. This psychic ability is called psychometry, a form of clairsentience. By formal definition, it is *the ability to discover facts about an event or person by touching inanimate objects associated with them.*

I was too young when I became aware of that empathy I was experiencing. I didn't even know how to express what I was feeling. My family, devoutly Christian, were members of a faith that ill-prepared us to accept the concept of psychic connections. In any event, there would have been little information available to us about psychic abilities – and I was only a small child when it all began.

Back to 1963: On a particular day in August, I was playing in the kitchen near the fire escape window, which was wide open. In the outdoors background, someone was playing the song *Up on the Roof* by The Drifters. It was a big hit that year. As I was playing, I began to feel a bit heavy, like something strange had come over me. It didn't feel bad exactly, just somewhat oppressive. Of course, as a child, I couldn't have described it even if I had wanted to confide in anyone. The energy stayed around me, and I felt something strange on the top of my head, a tingling feeling.

Later, I learned that it was my crown chakra reacting. I know now what spirit energies feel like. As a medium, I have experienced them many times.

11

At one point, I was looking toward the living room from the kitchen, and I became aware of a type of radar within myself. Suddenly, my eyes grew large and intensely focused. I saw an apparition; to my young eyes, it was a monster. The specter appeared to be heading in the direction of the hospital not far from where we lived. It seemed to be hurrying. (Was it on its way to pick up a soul?) The hooded robe it wore was transparent; I could see straight through it. I now believe that our apartment just happened to be in its route. The specter walked into the wall and that was it; it was completely gone. After it left, so did the heavy energy and the tingle on the top of my head.

I couldn't believe it and yet, I had really witnessed it. Today, I associate this apparition's look to how the movies depict the Grim Reaper. I refer to it in the same way throughout this book. I have a feeling to this day that this "Reaper" is still on its same route, doing its business – whatever that is.

With my father gone, there were seven of us. We had only one television, and my older siblings constantly fought over it. Everyone wanted to watch something different. I, being the youngest, stayed out of the argument. I didn't have a say in anything; I knew I wouldn't have a chance at getting my way. Sometimes the conflict over the TV and other scant resources got physical.

My mother was depressed. Even for so loving a mother as mine, living with so many people in that small apartment was often unnerving and depressing; mom was overwhelmed. Sometimes she just let us do as we wished. She didn't always have the strength to give us the close supervision we needed.

A Breath of Fresh Air

When I was around seven years old, I heard from some of

the kids in the neighborhood that they were going to summer camp. I asked if I could go too. Feeling the need to alleviate our cramped conditions, mom decided yes, I could go. She thought that it would be good for me to get away from the city and our crowded conditions for a while.

The program was called the *Fresh Air Fund*. I stayed with a family called the Delavans in Syracuse, in upstate New York, for two weeks. It was my first experience living in the country. I loved it there. My mother had no idea how positive it was for me. It gave me a perspective in life that I hadn't had before. The country made me feel lighter and my head felt clearer. I didn't know I was psychic at that age, but still, I definitely was aware of a huge difference.

The Delavans were a well-to-do family. They weren't rich, but to me, it seemed that they were. Donald and Sonja were the parents. They had a daughter, Sabina, and two boys, Tom and Tim. They had two dogs: a very wild German shepherd named Dukee and another mixed breed called Toppy. The family lived in two different houses during the years I spent time with them. The first was a pretty light blue color and sat on some acreage where we roamed, ran, and played to our hearts' content. The second house was white and it sat on the top of a hill. Mrs. Delavan had always wanted a house on a hill, and Mr. Delavan fulfilled her dream. It was much larger and had many more rooms than the first house. I loved that house! It had a lot of land and it was away from other houses. There was a wooded area in the back where we used to camp out sometimes with small tents and sleeping bags.

They liked me so much that they asked if I could stay for another two weeks. I, of course, yelled out "YES!" Every summer for the next seven years, I visited the Delavans. I couldn't wait for school to end so that I could head to the country. Once summer began, I would go to Grand Central

13

station on 42nd Street in Manhattan and hop on the Amtrak train.

They used to introduce me as "our fresh air boy," and I would just smile and think, "I *am* fresh air." Mr. Delavan used to tell his three children, "Freddie is with us because he is less fortunate than we are." As if the kids knew what that meant! I didn't feel that way at all, and I *did* know what it meant! I loved the Delavans. They showed me a way of life that I wanted. It was the "American Dream." Back then, I thought that living in a house in the country was the ideal way to live. I especially loved feeling so light and free of the dark impressions in the building at home. I loved the country back then. So much has changed with the gradual development of my understanding and acceptance of who and what I am. Today, when I visit my cousins in upstate New York, I get bored and want to return to the hustle and bustle of the big city!

Once, the Delavans asked me if I wanted to live with them permanently. Mr. Delavan told me I would be able to visit my mother and call her any time I wanted. I was tempted and grateful, but I said no. No amount of money, luxuries, or the country, was going to keep me away from the "less fortunate" family that I loved. We didn't have much, but we had each other. Besides, my mom would never have agreed to that. There are those who have money and are very happy because they also have love, but there are also those who have everything except love and happiness. The Delavans, at that time, were a close-knit and loving family, and I shall always be grateful that they shared a part of that love with me.

I stopped going there as the Fresh Air Fund kid when I was 14 years old. After that, I went back to visit and spend time with them on my own. I just bought an Amtrak train ticket and went. I only stayed for two weeks. At age 16, I stopped

14

going at all, but I kept in touch. One day when I called, just to say hello, Mr. Delavan answered the phone. I knew immediately that something was different, since it had not been his habit to answer the phone. I was surprised and sorry to hear Mrs. Delavan had divorced him. I lost track of them altogether after that until I found their two sons, Tom and Tim, on Facebook in 2013.

Damaging Phenomena

I had been a talkative kid at six, but gradually I changed. My life was flooded with continuing strange occurrences that I did not understand. I was frightened by them; they were unsettling when they occurred, and afterward I would be extremely confused and uneasy. I wouldn't talk to anyone about what I was going through. I did not dare because I feared being made fun of, or worse, that I would be put away somewhere – perhaps an asylum for the mentally disturbed.

The impressions that surrounded us in the tenement were not the only ones I was enduring. Due to my father's drinking problem, there were negative energies all around us. I believe these energies had attached themselves to him; an experience I will share with you later.

More and more I became aware of how other people affected me. Because of being empathic, when someone felt happy, I felt happy. When someone felt sad, I became overwhelmed with emotion and sadness. Being around large numbers of people or crowds exposed me to a mixture of all kinds of emotions. At first, I had assumed this was what everyone experienced; I never questioned it. I was devastated to learn that I was different – different in ways I could not trust others to understand or accept.

During Christmas of 1963, I was playing with my toys when suddenly, I felt the energy again. I felt a whoosh behind me. I turned to see what it was, but it was gone. I knew what was there, though. The *"Reaper"* had paid a visit again; chills ran up my spine. I was a six-year-old psychic medium, and I didn't even know what that was.

I turned seven in January 1964, and it was around that time that the events occurring in my life changed: they became more intense. They were new and different; this was the hardest time of my life.

While in school, I continued to be subjected to unexplained energies. Random images of people I had never met or seen would appear in my mind. I wouldn't be thinking of anything or anyone at the time; they would just appear.

I also heard voices. This was my *clairaudient* abilities (the power to hear things outside the range of normal perception) coming into play. Some spirits would shout my name: "FREDDIE!" or, at times, the name of someone else. Other times, they would ask me to tell something to a student near me. For example, they might say: "Tell Johnny that Uncle Steve is here." Of course, I didn't say anything to Johnny because there was no one there, just words, coming from nowhere. If I had repeated anything to him, he would have looked at me strangely and warned others that I was "weird."

It is said that everyone has these abilities, but most have blocked or denied them at a young age and no longer recognize them. Some are, or remain, more aware of them than others and are able to experience them to a much higher degree. I tend to agree with this. A psychic can become a medium sometime in their life, or they can be born with abilities already fully functioning. A medium has to be psychic, but a psychic may not be a medium. Actually, when referring to these "abilities," I prefer the term *gifts* because everything that comes from God is a gift. I am not special in any way. I am but one medium among millions.

I recall lying on my bed one night; everyone else was asleep. It was dark, but the moon was out; its light shone softly into our living room. I began to feel a heavy energy around me. This energy was a bit different than what I had experienced in the past; it was very strong. I had felt energies before, like the *Grim Reaper's*, but it wasn't intrusive like this one. The *Reaper's* energy just came and left. This one wanted more; this one wanted to get my attention. Suddenly I heard someone call my name. The voice was a male and it had a Spanish accent. "Fredi, Fredi," it called to me. It wasn't a call I heard with my ears; I heard it in my head, clairaudiantly.

I turned in my bed to face the living room, and froze. My eyes were transfixed, my whole body became rigid and taut; I was afraid to blink or even to breathe. I wanted to run away and hide under the bed, but I couldn't move. A rush of heat ran throughout my body and I began to tremble. There, sitting on our living room chair was an apparition; it was a ghost, if you will. But again, I only saw a monster. Whatever it was, I knew it wasn't a flesh-and-blood person. It wasn't solid; I could see right through it.

Finally, with very slow and careful movements, my heart pounding as though it would burst out of my chest, I was able to cover my head with the blanket. I lay there, shaking, terrified. As the night passed, I was finally overtaken by weariness and slipped slowly into a fitful sleep. I kept waking up, still very frightened. I finally worked up the nerve to peek from under my blanket; it wasn't there anymore. I was so relieved!

When I woke up the next morning, I was still shaken. I couldn't wait to leave for school and get out of that apartment! The only problem was, it was Saturday. That meant I wasn't going to school and I was trapped there in those rooms where I felt especially exposed and vulnerable to whatever energies were around me.

I went to my mother, and I pointed to the chair where the ghost had sat the night before. I told her in Spanish what had happened. She responded by saying, "Don't be silly; no one was sitting on that chair last night, we were all in our beds, sleeping. There is no such thing as ghosts; you had to be dreaming."

I became emphatic. I told her I hadn't been dreaming! I had been fully awake! Of course, she didn't believe me and as I continued to insist I was telling her the truth, she began to shout at me: "What is wrong with you, why are you talking like that?"

I stopped speaking right in the middle of my desperate plea and realized why she was shouting at me. I was stuttering and I hadn't even noticed. "Stop talking like that!" she yelled. I could see that she was concerned and frightened as she pulled me to her and held me. Even when she yelled at me, my mom always made me feel safe. Unfortunately, the damage was done.

After that weekend, I returned to school as a stutterer. It was hard for me, since I had never stuttered before. Everyone thought I was playing around and the kids would yell out at me: "STOP STUTTERING!" I felt ashamed and confused about not being able to communicate as I always had. I shut down completely. I never raised my hand in class when the teacher asked a question, and I never asked any questions, as I had used to do. I prayed the teacher wouldn't choose me to stand up and answer a question. I noticed that I got stuck on certain words, so I would avoid using them. I had to be quick to pick another word in its place. It was hard to do that sometimes.

What I saw in my night of terror affected me in a way that changed my life forever. The trauma of seeing the ghost, which I thought might have been my father, affected me so much that the stuttering remained and became severe. What I have never understood is: If it was my father, why would the ghost feel menacing to me? I thought: *It had to be someone or something else.*

After that night, my mediumistic ability was a bit blocked. I unknowingly stunted it because of my frightful experience. I didn't see any more unknown people in my mind's eye or any more spirits with my *physical* eyes. This ability doesn't truly go away, of course, as I found out, but for the time being it was put on hold. My empathic ability continued very strong. This wasn't particularly upsetting to me because I still thought that everyone experienced the same thing.

Menacing Occurrences

In 1967, when I was 10 years old, I got a part-time job as a salesperson working at a woman's clothing store after school. It was in an open-air market on Park Avenue called *La Marqueta* (The Market). The place was huge. It began on 110th Street and went all the way to 116th Street and continued spreading out, left and right, for a few more blocks. I became an excellent salesperson. It was easy for me to know what the customer wanted because unknowingly, I was tapped into the way they felt. My employer loved the customer service I gave and that I was bilingual.

While I was growing up, there were two languages spoken in our household: Spanish and English. Since I was educated in English, as were my brothers and sisters, it was the language I best understood and used. We spoke Spanish only to our mom or other family members who were not fluent in English. For the first time, I was seeing what an advantage that could be in the real world. I was paid $30 every Saturday, which was a lot of money for a kid at that time. My income reduced my mother's expenses by quite a bit because I could buy my own clothing and contribute a little to the household.

La Marqueta was exactly that — a huge arena filled with stands of merchandise. Any item you might be looking for could be found somewhere, at one of the stands. Working at a clothing stand rather than in an enclosed building was hard on me during the winter. It got extremely cold, and sometimes it seemed unbearable. Any distraction from the cold was welcomed.

While I worked there, the Hare Krishna folks used to hold their chant rallies across from the clothing stand. While they were there, I felt a lot of energy — good energy. Sometimes I saw a glow radiating from them. Later in life, I learned I was viewing their "aura." An aura is a field of delicate, incandescent energy encircling a person or entity (as you would recognize a halo or aureola in a religious depiction). The formal definition is: *an invisible emanation produced by and surrounding a person or object: discernible by individuals of super normal sensibility.*

That same year, while I was working at *La Marqueta*, I got really sick. I had gone out to buy a bag of potato chips. I loved potato chips, and back then, twenty-five cents could get you a large bag. On my way home, as I was reaching the corner of 107th Street, I felt a bad energy. The energy felt heavy and intrusive. I inhaled something that I can only describe as the stench of rotten eggs. Today, I know it as *sulfur*. I have smelled sulfur as an adult, and sulfur or rotten eggs or excrement smells are usually associated with malevolent entities. I looked on the ground to see if there was something rotten, but there wasn't anything there. The odor was nauseating.

Once I got home, I ate my chips and watched television. By the time I went to bed, I felt ill. I kept tossing and turning and endured cold chills throughout the night. In the morning, I had a fever of 103. My mother was frantic with worry. She did all that she could to bring the fever down. She questioned me: "How could this happen?"

I told her about the foul smell I had inhaled, and she wondered, "How can a bad smell make you this sick?"

"I don't know, it just did," I answered. I was so sick that my mother finally took me to the hospital. The doctor told her that if she hadn't brought me in, I could have died. They explained to my mother that a fever of 105 and above could kill, and my fever had been heading toward those levels. They were uncertain about why I got such a fever. I wasn't ready to cross over yet. When it's your time to go, it's your time to go. That *Grim Reaper* wasn't going to take me yet.

There may be some connection to the fact that at the same time all of this was happening, heroin addiction was sweeping the streets of every major city in the United States. It was a huge problem in my neighborhood. Today I know how negative the energies are that attach themselves to heroin junkies and alcoholics. The mayhem that reigned in our streets was so bad that the adults in our community had to act to protect us from it. We were extremely fortunate to be looked after wisely.

Ghostly Hangouts

After I recovered from my illness, we went to see *The West Side Story*. They were playing it again. I hadn't had a chance to see it the first time; I was too young. Imagine, back then it was only a dollar to get in! There weren't many movies with Puerto Ricans or Hispanics in them in those days; the roles they did get were insignificant. When this epic film, depicting life in Spanish Harlem, became a major film, everyone in the Hispanic community wanted to see it again and again. We weren't called Hispanics in those days, either; that description came later.

While sitting there in the theater, I suddenly felt very uncomfortable. I felt as though someone or something was right up in my face; I began to feel ill and confused. My senses were in an elevated state.

You know the uncomfortable feeling you get when you "feel" that someone is staring at you, and when you turn to look, they are? Those are our psychic abilities at work. We all have those abilities; just some of us have them to a higher degree. I was sensing spirit energy. I enticed it, attracted it. Spirits know when an individual can sense them and they are drawn to it. Once I got out of the theater, I began to feel better.

Today when I know I am going to the theater, the library, or any other crowded place, I ground, center, and shield first. Barefooted, I stand in the middle of my living room. I take one crystal in each hand and I raise my forearms, palms up and open. I close my eyes and I imagine myself in a park on a beautiful sunny day. I am standing barefoot on the grass and I begin to imagine that roots are growing out of the bottoms of my feet, and into Mother Earth. I stay focused on this visualization for about 15 seconds. Then I begin to pay attention to my whole body. I relax my body and center my thoughts for about 30 seconds. Then I begin to shield myself, and say softly, "My Dear Lord God, Jesus Christ of Nazareth, my Angels and Spirit Guides, please fill my home with your beautiful clear pure white light, and shield me with a pure clear white light bubble." I continue standing there for another 30 seconds, and then I say, "Thank you, and amen."

There are places that earthbound spirits frequent more than others; buildings such as theaters, libraries, and places that have commotion and activity on a regular basis. They need the energy; it is food for them. It allows them to do things such as move a chair, or slap the popcorn, or drink out of someone's hand. They need an awful lot of energy to manifest enough for someone to see them. Some just want to be noticed because they are lonely or need help. Most earthbound spirits are not malevolent. People who don't go into the light immediately at death were usually good people in physical life, and that being their nature, they will not do evil deeds in spirit form.

For whatever reason, many buildings in New York City are frequented by spirits that didn't go into the light when they passed. Miriam and her family lived in an apartment on Amsterdam Avenue. They had two children; my beautiful nieces Linda and Rebecca. My sister Abby and I used to take the bus to visit them.

Miriam was certain her apartment was haunted; she felt a presence there. She would feel and even see a presence from the corner of her eye. When she turned to look, there wouldn't be anything there. She sensed it was a male. When I visited her there, I felt a very heavy negative energy; it felt as though it was an entity that was in some sort of pain. I felt uneasy, like I was being watched. When we would sleep over at Miriam's, I would have nightmares and sometimes see shadows. I felt it, but whatever was there didn't harm anyone.

It just made everyone aware that it was there. If my mediumistic ability was still as active at the time, (my frightening experience that had made me stutter still hindered me), I think I would have seen it. My empathy picked up on its sadness, I felt it was a spirit that hadn't been happy while alive and had committed suicide. If I had only understood then about the operation and purpose of my *gifts*, I would have tried to help the spirit go into the light. Even out of the physical realm, and into the next, spirits maintain free will and would go only if they desired to do so. Needless to say, my sister was happy to move out of that apartment.

New Energies and a Farewell

Finally a larger apartment was available for rent in the same building that we were already living in and the landlord let my mother have it. Apartment 27 was just one flight down from apartment 31, but from a paranormal point of observation, it was like moving miles apart. Apartment 27 was so much clearer; there was far less energy moving throughout our new home. In our new apartment, my brother Augustine, whom we called "Agun," and I had our own room with twin beds. Still, it was bittersweet to move from the only home I had lived in since birth. Yes, we were crowded there and experienced the things we had gone through there, but I will never forget apartment 31. One day I will go back there and ask if I can go inside for a bit. I would like to see if the *Grim Reaper* is still there, and running his usual route.

I was fifteen years old, when my grandmother Jovíta crossed over and my mother took me with her to Puerto Rico. I wasn't expecting to see what I was going to see when I got to my Aunt Gloria's apartment, which was also where my grandmother had lived. My aunt didn't have much. We were poor here, in Spanish Harlem, but compared to their dire straits, we were doing well.

24

My grandmother's casket was in the living room, and again there was the smell of flowers that reminded me of death. While I was sitting in the living room where the casket was, I felt a presence come to me and it remained with me during our entire stay there. It wasn't a bad energy, but instead, it felt loving and warm to me. I felt like it was embracing me. Being around a casket all day, for three days, was very strange for me, but I was filled with the sense of understanding, and it didn't frighten me at all. The flowers that I had hated as reminders of death when my father passed didn't bother me anymore either.

Some spirits don't communicate immediately after they cross over, but most do. I feel that when someone dies a traumatic death, they need time to heal on the other side. Some decide not to go into the light right away. Sometimes they have unfinished business or they have been murdered or committed suicide, or they are afraid of judgment. There are many reasons. I know that my grandmother did go into the light. I can feel her today, at times, especially when I am around my mother.

When I am giving mediumship readings, the spirits that come to me are those that have crossed over into the afterlife. I see them, feel them, and hear them. Someone once asked me, "When you do that, does it hurt? How does it make you feel?" I told him, "No, it doesn't hurt, usually." At times, the spirit wants to show me rather than tell me, depending on the skills that particular spirit has learned to communicate with. I might feel chest pain when the spirit is making me feel that he or she died with something related to the chest area. For instance, it could have been a heart attack or lung cancer, but I eventually get the cause. Even though I might feel chest pain, it's not extreme. The spirit doesn't want to hurt me, and if I feel uncomfortable, I just tell the spirit "Okay, I got it, you can stop now," and they do.

The day we buried my grandmother was very sad. Everyone was crying and I felt the emotional drain. This was the first time I had been to a cemetery. The day was stifling hot. We were all gathered around the burial site and the pastor began to give his sermon. I felt strange again standing in the plethora of energies around me. These energies didn't feel like live human energies though; I feel the difference between human and spirit energy.

When I walk into an empty room, I can feel that there were people there. Their energies are lingering like a residue, and I can feel their emotions. Some mediums say there aren't any spirits in cemeteries. Why should they be there when there are no physical beings? There is no energy for them to draw on. I feel there are no *ascended* spirits, spirits that have gone into the light, that frequent cemeteries. I do feel, however, that there are spirits that haven't gone into the light that frequent them. People have the preconceived belief of "ghosts in cemeteries" and have given it power. The spirits are more than happy to accommodate one's beliefs.

As time went by, I learned how to deal with the stuttering. I knew when to talk and when not to. I learned to work around it, aware that it worsened when I felt under pressure or nervous or when I had to talk to someone with authority. Because of my ever-present empathy, it would also reveal itself based on how people around me were feeling. I couldn't be around crowds because there would be people who were sick, depressed, and every other imaginable emotion or condition. In retrospect I see that I also learned how to control my empathy, just as I had learned how to work with the stuttering, even though I was unaware of what it was. This is how I progressed through grammar school, junior high, and then high school. Junior high was the hardest. I hated school and didn't want to go; children can be so cruel at times. And too often, adults are not prepared to make the necessary difference.

Like all things, Junior high eventually came to an end in June of 1973. I never wanted to set foot in that school again. Then high school really solidified the hatred I had for school; I didn't want to go. Sound familiar? I was about to drop out; the school was overcrowded, the teachers didn't care, and it was full of gangs. Through all of this, even though I struggled daily, I managed to keep my grades up. My grades were so good I qualified for a school called Park East H.S. just a few blocks from home. It was an experimental high school that worked with credits like a college. After a certain amount of credits, I would acquire my high school diploma. I loved the school and if I did well; I could graduate in two years instead of three. This blessed relief came just in time!

My homeroom teacher was Mrs. Kotterler, but she let us call her Jen. She was also the school's art teacher. She cared about us, and I believe that that is why I became so interested in art. Jen was Japanese-American and a very nice lady. I noticed that in that school the teachers were different. They were more "hip" and the students mattered to them. I was into photography and silk-screening, and for the first time, I became one of the popular students in school. I was "the artist."

Zulma

When I was-sixteen, a friend of mine introduced me to his aunts, Zulma and Jennie. They lived in a project apartment on 103rd Street and Third Avenue. Jennie was my age and Zulma was in her twenties. We became good friends. They had a sense of humor and always made me laugh. Jennie's laugh was, and still is, contagious. She was only sixteen, but it is apparent to me now that she had an old soul. It was the disco era, and every weekend we went out dancing. While we practiced our dance moves, Jennie choreographed it. We became quite good at doing the "Hustle," and dancing became one of my favorite things to do. I don't do much dancing anymore, but I can still "cut a rug."

During this time, I started to drink. We always started our evening with a shot or two — only enough to spark up our disco venture. After all, we wanted to be at our best! Jennie and Zulma were like sisters to me. Even so, there was something about Zulma's energy that I didn't really understand.

After helping her paint her apartment one evening, I spent the night; it wasn't a good idea to travel back home from the Bronx late at night. Zulma's son was staying with his grandmother and Aunt Jennie, so we were by ourselves, and Zulma began to open up to me.

She shared that sometimes when her son was eating and she was in the other room, she would peer into the kitchen just to check on him and when she did, she would often see what must have been an apparition of a Native American sitting at the table with him. She stopped talking after this revelation, looking expectantly at me, not really knowing how I was going to respond to her unusual disclosure.

All I could think was that the feeling I had about her made sense now and, although I really had no understanding of what it was I was sensing back then, I could only think: *Wow, I saw a Grim Reaper, and a ghost, and now, Zulma has seen a Native American. We definitely have something in common.* We had something mutual to share that evening. I told her about my experiences as a child; she was gifted like me.

28

Zulma chose not to develop or use her gifts. I feel that was because in the Puerto Rican community, and in some other Hispanic cultures, when a person displays these kinds of abilities, they are automatically linked to Santeria or a negative occult and are ostracized. She never learned anything about spirit guides, psychic abilities, or mediumship. She thought the Native American she saw with her son was evil, but the truth is that he was her son's protector, his spirit guide.

Some people believe that all protector spirit guides are Native Americans, but I don't believe that to be true. A protector spirit guide can be any loving spirit, maybe a family member who has crossed over. It can be one who is ascended or a spirit that didn't go into the light, or one who is earthbound. Many people refer to them as ghosts. A mother who dies and leaves children behind might not go into the light, thinking that she can't protect her children if she goes. But the truth is that as an ascended spirit, she will have more power than an earthbound spirit would ever possess.

Zulma was murdered about ten years ago. Someone hit her over her head with a shovel and left her for dead. She was in a coma for some time, and then crossed over. I miss Zulma. She was a good friend. I feel her sometimes, and I know that she did cross over into the light.

Chapter Two
A Sea of Empathy

"We live in a culture that discourages
empathy. A culture that too often tells
us our principal goal in life is to be rich,
thin, young, famous, safe, and
entertained." – *Barack Obama*

In February of 1975, I had enough credits to graduate from high school. Even though I was graduating six months early, all I could think was: *Finally!*

There was no graduation ceremony, but I didn't care; I was just relieved and happy that my years in high school were over. Now that I think about it as an adult, I wouldn't have minded wearing a cap and gown and having graduation portraits taken. Instead, I have only the memory of being handed my diploma. It's just the typical sort of regrets that we endure as adults. There are always things we wish we had done differently when we were younger.

Since I didn't have to wait until June to graduate and I had my diploma in my hand, I went home feeling like a weight had been lifted off of my shoulders. There were a few neighbors near my building's front stoop. "I did it. I graduated from high school!" I proudly announced. Everyone there looked at me with astonishment — during that time many kids dropped out of school; that's why my neighbors were amazed. It was a big accomplishment for me because of the problems I had with school; I hadn't thought I was ever going to graduate.

I ran eagerly upstairs. My sister Abigail opened the front door. "Look, I graduated!" I said, waving my diploma back and forth.

She was so happy that she hugged and kissed me. My mother, hearing our ruckus, wondered what was going on and came into the living room looking worried. "What happened?" she wanted to know.

"Freddie graduated from high school!" Abby shouted. "He got his high school diploma!"

My mother was so proud of me; she began to cry tears of joy. "We have to celebrate!" she said, and went to prepare my favorite food. It was *Arroz Con Gandules and Pernil,* that is, rice with pigeon peas and roast pork.

After things calmed down, I needed to spend some time thinking about what I wanted to do. Since I didn't have to be in class anymore, I slept later than usual. *What can I do with a high school diploma?* I pondered. The only thing I could think of was to get more education; just having a high school diploma wasn't enough for me to get a good, well-paying job. I was determined not to get stuck working in one of those fast-food places that require no marketable skills and pay only a minimum wage. Also, I knew I really wanted a place of my own.

I found an apartment on Lexington Avenue between 97th and 98th Streets. It was way up on the top floor and had no elevator — a scene that was all too familiar for me. It reminded me of when we lived in apartment 31, where the Grim Reaper used to make his appearance.

In the beginning, I liked my one-bedroom apartment. It had a large living room, a bathroom, and a small kitchen. The wood floors had an appealing shine. This was the first space I could claim as my own; I was happy with it. But then it began to feel eerie to me. I always felt that I was being watched. My psychic abilities were warning me.

I found a job at a men's clothing store. I was grateful to have the income, but I knew I was more creative than that. I had more to give and I wanted more out of life; I longed for the American dream. I really didn't like working as a sales person anymore, but it paid the rent, and I was able to save money. I took the position.

The clothing store was on 3rd Avenue, two blocks from my apartment. The two men who owned it were orthodox Jews from Israel. I knew they weren't from my neighborhood because they always spoke of their homes in Queens. They had been open for about five years and sold their merchandise at low prices. It was a one-room store with front windows that were used as showcases. The place needed a paint job. Both owners smoked cigars, so you were always hit by the smell when you entered the store.

I really disliked working at the clothing store because they always had me standing outside the door, trying to get people to come inside. It was cold standing out there for hours at a time. There were two other male employees in their twenties. I felt they were privileged. They weren't stuck out in the cold as I was, as the newest guy there. It was often 20 to 30 degrees out there! But I had to pay the rent, bills, and buy food, so I just endured. I wanted to go to college, but I didn't have enough money. Financial Aid only gives you a portion of the cost of tuition. I didn't want to go into debt before I had a good job, and I knew I would have to pay back any loans I took out. I felt trapped in this low-paying job — a job I didn't even like. I was miserable there, dealing with choosy customers who were often very difficult. I didn't enjoy selling anymore, as I had when I was younger in *La Marqueta.*

Evicted by Evil

As time went by, the apartment started to feel more and more uncomfortable to me. I felt a strong energy, a presence, there. Still, it wouldn't reveal itself to me. Having experienced the Grim Reaper and the apparition I saw as a child, I knew that such things existed. What I didn't know was that I felt these energies to a higher degree than most people because of my psychic abilities.

It was a powerful and creepy feeling. You know, it's like when you suddenly feel as if someone is watching you and you turn to look, but no one is there. Sometimes the hairs on certain areas of my body would stand up. I began to have nightmares almost every night. It got to a point that I didn't like being there at all. Sometimes, when I went to bed, my crown and third eye chakras went wild. I didn't know what it meant, so I tried my best to just ignore it. My stomach was always in a state of upset. It didn't occur to me immediately that this was due to my extreme empathy and I was just picking up the negative energies. I simply suffered the symptoms without knowing why. I am convinced that a person with undeveloped psychic abilities would not have noticed it as much. I felt that I was living in the presence of something evil.

Sometimes I would smell bad odors, like the smell of rotten eggs or old urine. Since I didn't cook, and the apartment was always clean, I couldn't figure out where those odors were coming from. At times, my crown and third-eye chakras would activate and I would feel a heavy tingle. In those days, I didn't know anything about chakras.

Objects began to be transported from one place to another around the apartment. I would put them in one place and they would show up somewhere else – or not at all. I lost my keys because they disappeared from the top of the refrigerator, where I always put them when I came home. I discovered *that* circumstance when I went to retrieve them so I could go to work and they were nowhere to be found. My toothbrush would end up in the middle of the living room. I would put water on low on the stove to make my coffee and return to find the pot sizzling and crackling on the burner; the water would be completely evaporated. Somehow the flame on the stove had been turned all the way up.

When it was evening time and the curtains were drawn, there was no light coming in. Yet I used to see a shadow moving around the apartment in different places – most often in the kitchen area or living room. Sometimes the shadow would be accompanied by the foul smell of a heavy concentration of urine that I mentioned before. One time I was sitting at the table eating my takeout dinner, and when I looked toward the living room I could see a large blob of a shadow moving slowly in the room. It stopped at the couch and lingered; then I saw the cushion push down and an indentation appeared as if someone had sat down. This made sense to me later when I saw an obese spirit there. I had seen him before.

The first time I saw the obese man, I was lying down on my hide-a-bed couch in the living room. Some time had passed and I was comfortable and relaxed, when I suddenly felt a very heavy energy. I had phased out of my body and into another dimension. It was the same dimension that the man was occupying, so I was able to see him. He sat at the foot of the bed, naked, and he looked powdery white. He was looking at me and he was laughing, a sinister laugh; his teeth looked dark and rotten. I had phased into a spirit dimension before and encountered spirits – but never like that one. I

35

didn't overreact. I actually felt some sense of relief because I knew now that what I had been feeling was accurate: the sensations I felt; the shadows I'd seen; the smells I had endured were all validated and the tingling warning of my chakras was "right on." They were all protective signals that something was nearby. I was just beginning to have some awareness of the spirit world and my connection to it.

Although I was relieved to find validation, I was also terrified. Some mediums are called trance mediums; they let their bodies be taken over by spirits. These spirits are usually master spirit guides, angels, or beings whose vibration is very high. They usually have a message to give to the world by using the trance medium.

I am not a trance medium; I am a mental or spirit medium. I call what I do "astral trance" because when I phase out of my body, I am not "physically" conscious, but I am very aware and I don't let spirits take over my body. I'm just not wired that way. Sometimes I communicate by astral trance. I am in the middle, connected to both worlds. I have one foot in the physical world and one foot in the spirit world.

When I saw the obese, naked man and realized this was the presence I had been experiencing, I quickly snapped out of my astral trance. The naked man was gone now, and I saw only white smoke or vapor in my apartment. I ran to see where it was coming from, and it was coming from a valve in the hallway about ten meters from my front door; it had burst. The vapor was everywhere – and thick. I looked and saw Jimmy, the building's superintendent, busy working at shutting it off. I didn't know much about him; I rarely saw him. But I was grateful to see him now. I was talking to him while he was fixing it. "I don't understand how this happened," he said in Spanish, as though to himself. He looked at me strangely and I could almost hear his thoughts: *I wonder if he had something to do with this.*

My abilities were right on target in feeling the way I did in that apartment. I went back inside, filled with concern — I was feeling fearful. I had thought that there was a fire. Everything in my psychic senses told me it was the obese spirit who was responsible for this. I knew that I did not want to live there anymore, not after what I had witnessed. It was as if the events in my life were pushing me to take note of my psychic strengths.

About a week after the whole broken valve incident, I told the building manager that I would not be renewing my lease.

The day finally arrived; I was moving out of there. I went down and told the building manager that I was leaving. I also told him that the door was open because I had lost my keys. When I had to go out, to go to the store or work, I had been forced to leave the door open ever since my keys disappeared. He said that was fine, and I left to go stay with my mother until I figured out what I was going to do next.

I was at the age when most young people don't know what to do with their lives. I knew everyone has a calling in life, and I was focused on figuring out mine. I had read that the average person is stuck in a job that they hate; I didn't want to spend my life that way. While I was young, other kids used to tell me: "I want to become a doctor..." or "...a lawyer when I grow up." That was the norm. There is nothing wrong with that, but I didn't want to be a doctor or a lawyer.

Many young people might choose those careers because that is what their parents expect or desire for them. I feel that a person who is born to become a doctor will care deeply about their work and will be the very best they can be at it. It is not a *calling* when it is a career choice that is made only for prestige, or title, or to please someone else. In my estimation of things, this brings up the matter of reincarnation.

Reincarnation is a fact to me. The spirit that will occupy our physical body upon our re-entry determines our calling. Before we come back to this earth plane, we make choices that will help teach us what we are coming back to learn. However, we forget these things we have chosen for ourselves upon our rebirth or shortly thereafter. I feel that there is a reason for that. We are beginning a whole new contract with God, with a clean slate. If we return only to continue where we left off, we won't learn any new lessons, or balance any karma that we might have accumulated in our past lives. Some people are so aware of their "higher selves" that they become cognizant of their calling very early in their lives. These people are often very happy and successful.

In the matter of my former apartment, I can only assume that the presence I encountered there had a great deal of karmic debt and lessons to learn! So I left the body-seeking, foul smelling, obese spirit to wander alone in the empty walls of the apartment.

I was again, temporarily, at my mother's place.

I was sitting in the living room on the couch watching television, when I heard a knock on the door. I got up and answered, finding two police detectives there. They wanted to speak to me and asked me to step out into the hallway. One of the detectives asked me what happened when I left the apartment on Lexington Avenue. I told them that I had finished moving out and told the manager that I had lost the keys for the door and then I left. One of the detectives told me that a fire had been started in the apartment. He asked me straight out, looking me in the eye: "Did you start a fire in that apartment?"

I was shocked! I was suddenly very uncomfortable and nervously replied: "No, I didn't start a fire in that apartment." I felt myself go hot and become flushed; I felt my heart drop. I didn't know where this was coming from or what was coming next.

"You told the manager that the door was open?" one of them asked.

"Yes I did," I said, "because I had lost my keys and couldn't lock the door." The detective looked at his partner, and I felt by the expression on their faces that they knew I didn't start that fire. If I had started the fire, I would have just left. I never could have done anything like that anyway. I would never harm anyone, except in self-defense or to protect another.

They told me they would investigate this further. They asked if I was going to live at my current address for a while; I answered that I would. One of the detectives gave me his card in case I learned anything regarding the fire. I took the card and looked at it. I thanked him and walked back inside without saying anything. I guess they must have closed the case; I never heard from them again.

I had a bad feeling in my gut about that fire, though, I'm sure, it was a paranormal phenomenon. I have a strong feeling that the entity I saw in that apartment became enraged because it could no longer attempt possession of me. I believe it started that fire. It was evil and destructive. My angels and spirit guides were protecting me as they always do. I feel that the entity was attached to that apartment or to the building and

39

couldn't leave it. If it could have left, I feel that it would have attached itself to me and followed me wherever I went.

I have a friend who moved into that building shortly after I left. I dreaded visiting him there because of the bad energies the building harbored. I didn't want to come in contact with that malicious entity again, ever. I did attempt to visit my friend anyway, but when I walked into that building, I instantly felt I was engulfed in a dark shroud. I froze up and from that point on I refused to go there again. I asked my friend to meet me somewhere else in the city instead. He wondered why. I told him I just didn't feel comfortable there. I didn't elaborate because I couldn't; how could I? I still didn't feel comfortable sharing what happened to me in that apartment. He didn't push it and we just started meeting elsewhere.

I still didn't know what I wanted to do with my life and I was feeling lost. I didn't know what direction to take. I realized that I needed to get away completely and find a path to follow.

A Daring Move

I was pondering this when I saw an army recruitment commercial on television. It was peacetime, but we were still in the cold war era. After that commercial, I was left with thoughts that kept repeating themselves in my head. I got up and started to pace back and forth.

My mom asked me "What is wrong with you?"

I told her about the commercial, and she told me that it was a bad idea. "What if a war breaks out?" she questioned apprehensively.

I didn't want to upset her, but I told her that I could save the money from the GI bill and go to school when I got out. I hugged her to make her feel better. I convinced her that it was a good idea. It already was to me. I didn't feel that we were going to war anytime soon. I felt deep in my soul that I was right; it turned out that I was.

Even though I felt confident in my decisions, I really gave it a lot of thought before I became an army recruit. My family didn't care for the idea because that meant I would be gone from them. Of course, I would miss them all, especially my mom. They did agree that taking one's right path in life is important. I really felt that this was the way for me to go. I understood that I wasn't going to get where I wanted to be in life anytime soon, but I knew this was one of the stepping stones that would move me closer to my goal.

Some of our neighbors in the building were in the army, so I asked them questions about their experiences. I was hoping to gain insight into army life, just in case it wasn't really the path for me. They advised me on the dos-and-don'ts, but they left out a lot of other information that would have *really* prepared me — I guess they didn't want to scare me.

After assessing the pros and cons, I went to the Armed Forces' office on 42nd Street; it was right in the middle of Times Square. I went inside to get some reading material on each military branch, and I filled the bag they gave me with all kinds of pamphlets. When I got home, I began to do my homework. The Marines were too gung-ho for me; I get sea sick, so the Navy was out. I didn't feel I could pass the Air Force test; so the Army was the one for me. My decision was made; I would do it.

Having decided to enlist, I went to the recruiting office to begin my new adventure as a professional soldier. I had to take a test to determine my IQ. I didn't score high, but I also didn't score too low. I wasn't very educated and I knew that, so I was pretty open to what would be available to me. I was only 19, and very green behind the ears — a deep fluorescent green to be exact. I did have the advantage of having been raised in New York City, where street smarts are a must; I could get along with a lot of different people. I found that those who were raised in rural areas, where the majority was of the same race and cultural backgrounds, weren't as tolerant of the diversity that military life brings.

The staff sergeant, who was giving the test, called me in and asked me to sit down. He asked me, "Do you like going out camping?"

It didn't take me long to answer. I said: "I love camping!"

He said, "Excellent, I have the perfect Military Occupational Specialty (MOS) for you. You can become a professional soldier in the Infantry, an 11 Bravo." I agreed to that idea without any hesitation. This could easily have turned out to be one of the biggest mistakes I have made in my life. I immediately went into an MOS that provided training that really couldn't be used in civilian life – unless I was going to be a hit man.

Needless to say, I know it's not a surprise, I really got suckered in! That staff sergeant was so good at what he did; I didn't feel any deception from him at all. I am usually extremely empathic, adept at feeling deception; but maybe because I wanted it so badly, I just wasn't paying attention. Anyway, I was not fully cognizant at that time of what my senses could tell me. Thus I signed a chunk of my life away. Once my signature was on those papers, I could see the nice expression on his face quickly change to one of "I got you." I had no idea what I had gotten myself into. He gave me a paper that said I had to report to Fort Dix, New Jersey, on a specific date. I said thank you and goodbye. It was that simple and I was that naive.

Soon the date came for my departure. My mother and family were worried and sad. It was very difficult for me. I struggled to keep up a brave front as I fought back tears; hugged everyone and said my goodbyes. A military van picked me up at a designated area in the city. There were several other new soldiers already in the van. There was a sense of camaraderie as if we shared the thought, *Yep, we all did it, we all signed; now we're in this together*; the van moved forward and we were off to a military training base at Fort Dix near Trenton, New Jersey.

We arrived in Trenton at about 8 a.m. that morning. There were many recruits there waiting to be picked up. The soldiers working at this building looked at us as if they felt sorry for us; they certainly didn't envy what we were about to embark on. I noticed some huge trucks approaching the building. They were large, long, dark green trucks, designed more for carrying cattle or horses than for people. The truck beds were completely enclosed and had horizontal openings in the sides that were thin rectangles, just wide enough to give passersby a head view of passengers inside. They stopped and a few drill Sergeants got out. *"ALL RIGHT YOU GOOD FOR NOTHING MAGGOTS! PICK UP YOUR BAGS AND FORM A LINE RIGHT HERE, RIGHT NOW, AND MOVE IT!"*

Shocked and unnerved, we were all quick to fall in line. A voice that had begun asking, "Oh shit! What have I done?" got louder inside my head. Once we were all inside the truck, the doors were closed and it was soon very hot. We rode, packed in like sardines in a can, for over thirty minutes to get to our destination. We all just stared at each other, afraid to say anything. I was overwhelmed by all that was happening.

My empathy was getting the best of me. I felt *everyone's* fear, confusion, nervousness, anger, and every other emotion they were experiencing.

When the doors opened again, immediately we heard *"OK GIRLS* (us being all males)*, PICK UP YOUR BAGS, GET OUT OF THE TRUCK, AND FORM A LINE RIGHT HERE IN FRONT OF ME. NOW MOVE IT!"*

We got out as fast as we could; we were like a bunch of dogs with our tails between our legs, doing as our master bid us. We formed a line and the drill sergeant shouted *"PICK UP YOUR BAGS AND DO A RIGHT-FACE, YOUR MILITARY RIGHT!"* A few of the soldiers went to the left instead. His voice blasted us again: *"FORWARD MARCH!"* Some of the recruits had heavy bags, and we marched at a fast pace. Several guys dropped out because they weren't used to the exercise; they were out of shape, overweight or small in build. And yet again that penetrating voice rang out : *"HURRY UP, YOU MAGGOTS. CATCH UP!"*

Our march ended at a large new-recruit holding facility. Here we were given shots and all of our heads were shaved. We were checked out by medics. Our *TA-50* (Training gear & Materials) was issued to us. This consisted of the uniforms of 1979, army-issue green. The newer camouflage fatigues did not appear until 1981. We were given caps, boots, socks, and underwear; our army "dress greens" came later, nearer the end of training. They already knew that we were about to lose a lot of weight, so we had to be fitted into them as we got closer to the finish and graduation. That seemed a long road away at that moment.

Basic training was hard for everyone. But some of the would-be soldiers fell by the wayside; it was just too hard for them. Some were discharged for disorderly conduct. Others, and this always seemed a little troubling to me, were discharged because they were bed-wetters.

I often thought that I wasn't going to make it myself, but I kept on going. It was hard for me, not only because of the training, but because of my psychic abilities. I continuously felt confused, scared, hungry, tired, and sad. I knew that I was homesick and that added to my anxiety, but I also knew that every emotion everyone else was experiencing was magnified by ten for me. I kept picking up on what the other soldiers felt. I did make it, though, and graduation day finally came.

We had to look perfect because we were going to be reviewed by the top brass. Our shoes had to be spit-shined and we had to be able to see our reflection in the decorations we wore on our dress greens. We had to practice our march onto the graduation field; it had to be done by the number – in other words, flawless.

After two months of boot camp and with graduation behind me, I heartily welcomed a visit home. There, I could relax and take it easy for a short while. I was in really good shape and I looked good, so I was told; I actually turned some heads. I had lost some weight, had a very nice tan, and I was tight and toned from all the exercise and running I had done. I did party some; after all I was in New York City. I spent a lot of time with my family as well.

It felt like a weight had been lifted off me. Basic training was out of the way; I had done very well. I had made some friends while there too. A few of them were going with me to Fort Benning, Georgia. We were all entering the same two-month-long MOS 11 Bravo Infantry training.

My leave time was too short; all too soon I had to say my goodbyes again. It sure hadn't gotten any easier. In fact, it was even harder now because I knew what to expect and I had already heard that the Infantry training was tough. At least I was in shape this time; I knew the drill, so it wasn't going to be the surprise that basic training had been.

I also knew that I would be overwhelmed with the emotions of my fellow soldiers again. In some ways, that was the hardest part.

Fort Benning, Georgia, in 1979, was a beautiful place. The area was very green; the breeze would often carry the scent of fresh-mown fields in our direction. My platoon consisted of about 36 soldiers, and we were there to learn what it meant to be part of the Infantry. The Infantry is the primary land-combat force, the backbone of the Army. It is the role of the Infantry soldier to be ready to defend our country: to capture, destroy, and repel enemy ground forces whenever necessary.

To accomplish this noble goal, Infantryman training required 14 weeks of One Station Unit Training. This includes Basic Combat Training and Advanced Individual Training. Some time was spent in a classroom, but the rest was spent in the field. It was an extremely demanding curriculum. The toughest part was the forced march; we had to carry heavy rucksacks and our weapons for up to 10 miles at a time, with very little rest. I performed as part of a fire team during drills and combat; I aided in the mobilization of vehicles, troops, and weaponry. I also assisted in reconnaissance missions, surveying and exploring, investigating, and drawing out the enemy. I learned how to process prisoners of war and capture documents that can be used for intelligence.

Our days were long; they started hard and early. We were up at 4:00 a.m. We needed to be clean-shaven, with a clean barracks and in formation within one hour. Then we began our physical training, which included a daily 4-to-5 mile run.

Following all of that, we went back to the barracks to shower and dress in our combat gear. By 5:30 a.m., we were in formation again and heading for the mess hall to have chow — breakfast.

I met many soldiers in Georgia, but I made one friend in particular; his name was Quijano. Quijano was from a Puerto Rican background. He was short; about 5 feet tall, and with my 5 feet 10 inch frame, we were an interesting pair. The long marches, coupled with the heavy gear, were very hard on him. Somehow he managed; he never quit. He pushed through with grit and graduated with the rest of us. He had a great sense of humor and that gift made many a difficult time much easier to get through. His ability to make me laugh at the most *not funny* times really helped me to finish the training — not that I had a choice in that!

When you first enlist or reenlist, the military gives you some choices of where you would like to be stationed, although the final decision is theirs. They have bases all over the world, and those choices vary depending on which branch you enlist in. A soldier doesn't stay at one base for his or her whole enlistment contract. I enlisted for four years. I chose Germany because I wanted to get a taste of Europe, do some traveling, and further my education. After my MOS training, I graduated. I had a brief opportunity to go back home before I left for duty in West Germany for two years.

Again, I was saying my goodbyes and again tears filled my mother's eyes as I headed out to the airport. I didn't feel good about leaving her; I felt like I was abandoning her. I had a hard time shaking that feeling; it traveled with me for quite a distance. I reminded myself that grown children must make their own lives, whether it is near or far.

47

The Armed Forces have a specific section at the airport where military personnel assemble before their flight. There, the soldiers' papers are checked and immunizations records examined to ensure that they have had all of their required shots before they board the airplane. My papers were in order; soon I had boarded the plane and was on my way.

Being stuck on an airplane wasn't at all fun for me. I felt a concentration of fear that didn't make sense to me. I wasn't afraid to fly. When I used to go to Coney Island, I got on the most terrifying rides there, repeatedly. This time though, I felt gripped by fear. We hit some turbulence, and when that happened, the fear became so strong that I was thrown into a full blown panic attack. I realized that it was the accumulation of the fear I was feeling from everyone around me. I was picking up telepathically what others were thinking as well. I was seized by the thought: *I can't wait until we land!*

When we finally landed at the Frankfurt airport, I felt some relief, but I know now that it takes some time to shake energies off that are temporally attached to our aura field.

Overwhelming Sensations

It was 1980 and I had just landed in Germany. The Germans take great pride in their country and it shows. Everywhere I went when I was sightseeing, it was clean and well kept; there was a very pleasing sense of organization. Germans did not like having American soldiers in their country, though, and they were very open about it. We did not get a warm welcome into their establishments. Once I went into a bar in the town of Mannheim, and they asked me to leave simply because I was an American soldier. It was against the law to do that, of course, but who wants to be in a place where you're not wanted?

From the airport, we boarded buses going to several different army bases throughout West Germany. I had been assigned to the 8th Infantry Division called the Pathfinders. I was on my way to a base called Coleman Barracks or Coleman Army Airfield, located in the Sandhofen district of Mannheim.

The original airfield in Sandhofen had been rebuilt as the *Fliegerhorst-Kaserne in 1937* as a *Luftwaffe* (Nazi air army) base. It had been closed to the public and rebuilt.

After WW II until mid-1949, the area was used as a collecting point for unserviceable automobile material and for surplus storage. In 1951, a replacement depot was established at Coleman Barracks and served as the staging area for all troops arriving in Germany. Throughout its operation by the U.S. Army, rumors have circulated of an extensive set of tunnels beneath the airfield, under the base and a number of underground hangars behind the barracks of the Signal Corps units. The tunnels and other underground facilities were supposedly flooded after the war. In reality, these tunnels actually do exist. They extend for miles through the mountains. The Nazis dug them as a shortcut, so they wouldn't have to go over or around the mountains; they were put in place as a quick exit from the airbase if it was necessary.

There was an alley that ran behind a cluster of barracks located next to a pronounced slope where numerous bunker entrances were located, all of which were rumored to be locked. Despite the lack of any hard evidence that remains at the site, these rumors have persisted over the years and stories of hidden Nazi bunkers and underground tunnels are passed on from one generation of soldiers stationed at Coleman to the next. I have seen the original maps of these tunnels, and I am left with sobering thoughts of the laborers that were used to dig them. Today, as far as we know, there is no access to any of those. Coleman Barracks serves as an airport for U.S. generals and houses the Army's only military prison in Europe.

Since I was unmarried, I was made to live in the barracks; I had no choice in the matter. They were an eyesore, old, very dull and gray, not much green around them. The rooms were very small, and at times up to three soldiers shared one, that made for heavy tension among us. Our barracks was near a sewer that always reeked with a foul odor. They didn't have bathrooms with showers in the rooms; we had to go downstairs and use a latrine that had a large shower; more than one of us had to shower at a time. There were several toilets and sinks with mirrors; we had to crowd in together to shave. Shaving was important; we weren't allowed to have any facial hair.

My roommates were two African-Americans in their early twenties. Our small quarters were already crowded, but they also held three large lockers that made the room even smaller. I learned quickly that throwing young males who were filled with uncertainties into tight quarters could be trouble.

Robert was from Washington, DC, and the other guy, James, was from Atlanta, Georgia. It was obvious from the start that they were both coming from different worlds than the one I grew up in. The fact that they were Black wasn't an issue with me; I had grown up around African-Americans. I was blessed to be surrounded by multicultural influences my entire life. Racism is born out of fear of the unknown and sadly, they were both ignorant and racist. They teamed up together against me because I was Puerto Rican, or more likely, I wasn't Black. There was always some racial issue with them. The anger and dislike they had for non-Blacks was constantly aimed toward me.

50

James was into martial arts and walked around as if looking for a reason to fight all the time. Robert was a know-it-all who challenged everything I said. They were constantly disrespecting me and my small space in the room. I had finally made up my mind that I wasn't going to take any more abuse from them. Reason wasn't working; I knew I was being pushed farther and farther toward a territorial stand.

One night, Robert had his TV up loud and it was late, after lights out. We had to be up and ready for a new day in only a few short hours. My simple request for quiet was all it took. The fragile thread of civility, which had been holding tempers in check, unraveled – triggering a fist fight. The time had come for me to assert myself and I did. We pounded against one another for only a few minutes, in that small tight room. I must have gotten in the better punches, because from that day forward he showed me more respect.

I kept to myself around my roommates, from that day on. I had a lot of Black friends on post, and when I would tell them about Robert and James, they would tell me those guys were ignorant. It was a great relief to me when their rank changed and they moved into another room.

Segregation was standard in the military. The soldiers usually kept with their own race. It wasn't imposed on us, but it was an unspoken norm. In the mess hall, there was an unofficial White soldiers' area and the Black and Hispanic soldiers had tables where you weren't welcome if you weren't like them. But there were tables that were ethnically mixed as well, and I always sat there.

We were all Americans with a mission: to represent and protect our land and assist our allies around the world. Yet at the same time we were divided from within. My background is Puerto Rican, but since I was born and raised stateside, I found that even the Puerto Ricans from the island kept away from me. I guess they felt that I wasn't like them. I might not have been born in Puerto Rico, but my mother raised me as though I was; I ate the food, spoke the language, danced and listened to Salsa music, and followed all of our customs. But I was still seen as an outsider by the Puerto Rican islanders. I would hope that things have changed since 1979.

I was a very good runner in those days. When my battalion held a 20-kilometer marathon (about 13 miles), I entered my name to participate. I really hadn't considered that it was a very hot day, and I wasn't dressed in appropriate attire for the event. I soon found myself miserable and overheated, but I didn't back down. I ran the race at a steady pace; I just kept on going. I wouldn't and I didn't give up. As I was running, I noticed the onlookers were watching me with a lot of interest. It turned out that I was way ahead of the pack, with only a lieutenant in front of me. I kept looking at him; concentrating on getting closer to him. I almost caught up with him, but not quite. He, dressed in his racing attire, crossed the finish line just seconds ahead of me.

I received a second-place trophy in front of the whole battalion. It made me proud, and my whole platoon was proud of me. From that day on, I was treated with more respect. It's amazing what a run can do for your popularity. Ultimately I had reason to regret my success because from that point forward, I became the head runner on company runs; that means it was my job to get out ahead, to stop and watch out for vehicles.

I had been stationed and serving in West Germany for 22 months. I had two months left on my tour when the battalion leader decided we would take a field trip to Berchtesgaden, a municipality in the German Bavarian Alps. While there, we went to the *"Kehlsteinhaus"* (this translates as the *Eagle's Nest*), a chalet-style structure nearly 1.25 miles above the town of Berchtesgaden. It had been built as an extension of the Obersalzberg complex, erected by the Nazis and intended as a 50th birthday present for Adolf Hitler, to serve as a place for him to entertain visiting dignitaries.

There are a lot of residual energies in Eagle's Nest, and they aren't virtuous ones. Back then, I didn't understand about energies; I thought they were *just feelings* within me. But it was the association there that made me very edgy. Standing in the same place that Hitler stood was, to me, as though I was standing in filth. I was in a place where a living demon once walked. Demons rarely live a physical life, but Hitler was one of those demons who did. Spiritual demons are pure evil. If I had known then what I know now about myself, I would never have gone there — I strongly feel that he was born to destroy.

During our Berchtesgaden field trip, we also visited *Dachau Concentration Camp*. I wasn't very excited about going to Dachau. However, I must admit I was curious and my curiosity got the best of me. That was something I would regret very quickly — I wished I'd never gone.

I had imagined that I would be sad or angry or physically uncomfortable. I did feel all of those things at times, but more than anything, I just sort of felt numb. I managed somehow at the worst moments to detach mentally. The best way I can describe it is that I observed it as though I were on a movie set, as opposed to actually being in a concentration camp.

The tour began with a look inside the Memorial Building. It was very new and modern, with a bookstore and cafe. The photographs of the experimentation chambers made my hair stand on end. I wished I hadn't gone in. I realized that this was only the beginning of the impressions I knew awaited me. I was accustomed to maintaining control of my feelings, coping in silence with the impact of the surrounding energies, but I was about to encounter something I had never experienced before.

I am sure there have been other psychics who had traveled there who felt what I did. Some may have felt and seen even more. At that time in my life, I thought everyone felt what I did. I didn't ask specific questions from the others, though. The experience was so powerful it left everyone with an unspeakable feeling of horror. I know that everyone can feel energies if they are tuned in, but a sensitive psychic will feel those energies in a more literal, experiential way.

Once we were outside the Memorial Building, we could see the actual camp. My first reaction to what I saw was that it was accurate in terms of the image I had in my mind. It looked exactly as I had expected: the massive flatland in the middle of the barracks and buildings; the barbed wire fence surrounding the perimeter; the watch towers; and the main gate. Everything was all as I had imagined it to be.

The sheer size of the installation added to its impact on me. The camp itself occupies approximately 5 acres within the 20 acres where the SS barracks, factories, and other facilities surround the detention area. This was the first Nazi camp created for political prisoners — Jews, and other so-called "undesirables." To read and see everything in the museum building took me at least two hours. As morbid as this might sound, I felt compelled to go through the two crematoriums. There are heart-rending memorials to all the different groups of people that were affected, throughout the facilities.

At first, Dachau housed many prominent prisoners who came from political, artistic, academic, and noble backgrounds.

Later, when Hitler began the *Final Solution* — the Nazi plan to exterminate the Jewish people, Dachau became a camp strictly for Jews and other minorities from all over Eastern Europe.

Because Dachau was the first of all the camps, Dachau served as a prototype and model for the other Nazi concentration camps that followed. Almost every community in Germany had members taken away to these camps. By the end of Hitler's reign of terror, a network of over 40,000 facilities had been operating in Germany and within German-occupied territory.

During the time Dachau was in operation, the town' inhabitants turned a blind eye to what was going on right under their noses — and this happened everywhere throughout Germany; this is how the Nazis got away with so much. So, naturally, after the camp was liberated, the people were embarrassed. As a result, they tried to hide the camp. Most of the barracks were destroyed, a man-made hill was put in place, and trees were planted to enclose what was the most shameful part of the small city.

In later years, though, the city decided to embrace its culture rather than turning its back on history. Thus, the Memorial was built and it became a place for people to visit, to learn, and understand what had happened there. I was stunned by the amount of documentation the Germans had of all that had happened. I suppose that the evil demon, Hitler, wanted to make sure history recorded him as the savior of the "pure" race and demanded the documentation.

Walking through the building, in the same rooms where people had died and been cremated, was utterly horrific. It's something that I had seen in textbooks or in movies during history class. But to see it with my own two eyes, to stand where so much evil took place, was a feeling that I can't describe to you. It is a feeling that haunts you to your very core. My detachment became a little difficult once we entered this area.

I was engulfed immediately in the anguish, fright, and despair that permeated the very air of this place. Suddenly it was as though I had been transported through time; it was 1940s Germany, and I was there — literally.

The most difficult part came toward the end of the tour, when we went into the gas chamber. The original ovens used to cremate the bodies were still there, as well as the upgraded ones they used later. We learned that the people who were killed here were commonly brought from other camps. When asked to go in, they simply thought they were going in to be shaved and showered, just as they had in any other camp. I had never considered this before, but it seems less depressing than their knowing that they were going to die. Still, it was no less hideous.

The gas chambers were used more frequently toward the end of the camp's operational era because of disease and over-population. When the Dachau camp was liberated by U.S. troops on April 29, 1945, more than 200,000 prisoners had come through the gates, many thousands of those people died under harsh and appalling treatment.

It is estimated that more than 11 million people were killed during the Holocaust.

My mediumistic abilities were still blocked when I was in Germany, but I was struggling with my empathic ability. I felt the earthbound spirits around me. I felt energies; I can only describe my overwhelming feelings as deep and sorrowful. I know I could feel the grief of those taking the tour, but I am sure that I was absorbing the sadness from those poor souls that were still there as well. I saw what looked like shadows a few times when there was no one around creating them. Words cannot describe the kind of place this is. The feelings I had while walking around the area where torturous experiments were carried out on other human beings were surreal, to say the least. I could not fathom how any human being could inflict, and commit, such acts as those on other souls. But it really happened; while I was there, I lived it.

I heard the sounds of low voices filled with longing; I heard them with my inner ears, the ones inside my head. If my mediumistic ability had been active, I am sure I would have seen them as well; the atmosphere was heavy with a morass of residual emotional energies — the grim and the gray — squeezing against me, nearly making it impossible for me to move.

As we entered the outer courtyard, I saw what looked like a female form. She might have been in her thirties, with dark brown hair and a very thin, skeletal frame. She wasn't fully materialized and now I don't understand how I was able to see her. But as I mentioned before, if spirits want us to see them, we will – no matter who we are.

After that experience, I can most definitely ask, "Why should I be afraid of an earthbound spirit, or ghost?" I might feel fear at the thought that a neighbor could be a psychotic murderer. Someone we think we may know, or a stranger, can kill in a split second. This is what I tell people now; when they ask me if I am afraid of spirits, my answer is, "No, I am not afraid. I must admit I was afraid in the very beginning, but that went away after some time. I am more afraid of a physical being that could just kill me in cold blood.

Back in the USA

In 1981, I received orders to report to Fort Lewis, in Washington State. It was time for me to say my farewells to Germany; that was okay with me. I really didn't enjoy my tour in Germany; it left me with a residual of haunting memories – psychic and emotional. It wasn't what I thought it would be.

It was the dead of winter when I arrived at Fort Lewis. But the cold didn't matter to me. I found it refreshing and beautiful. It seemed to wash away all the negativity and the stench left behind in Dauchau and Coleman Barracks.

I found Washington State to be stunning! But I didn't like the weather — it rains, a lot. The people were friendly, and I made a few more friends while I was there. The base was huge, and our barracks were modern, unlike those in Germany. Getting around was easy there, too, even if you didn't have a car, like me. There was always some activity going on, like a battalion BBQ — all you could eat and plenty of beer.

In the summertime, when we trained in the fields, we could see the majestic forest around us and smell the pines and the earthy scent of the green moss that grew on their north sides.

Fort Lewis has been around a long time. It was originally established in 1917 and covered some 70,000 acres of land. I learned that this portion of prime prairie land, cut from the glacier-flattened Nisqually Plain, had been taken from the Nisqually tribe's original reservation.

Fire and Ice

While stationed there, I hoped to be promoted to a higher rank. In order for me to accomplish this, I had to become a very "strack" soldier, that is: I had to be strategically organized and combat ready. I had to take several training courses to develop myself into an outstanding soldier.

I was offered an opportunity to obtain a Jungle Expert patch in the jungles of Panama. I applied, and was accepted. I arrived in Panama in the summer of 1982, unaware that I would encounter a barrage of allergens. It was a nightmare for me! In addition, we were assaulted by all sorts of mosquitoes, bugs, and arachnids. There were species I didn't know existed; not everything that comes out of the Rain Forest is exotically beautiful after all.

Panama's jungle is home to an abundance of tropical plants, animals, and birds. Some of them can be found nowhere else in the world. But in spite of being ensconced in this land of plenty, it wasn't a very good experience for me. First, I am not at all a hot-weather person. I found the climate to be stifling. In addition, the military training jungle was entirely unappealing; I really couldn't find much beauty in it. I knew that in other parts of Panama, where the jungles were undisturbed by Army activities, they were far more interesting. This place hardly warranted the glory implied by the title "jungle," I actually saw a lot of garbage on the "jungle" grounds. The place was littered with Army-issued canned food containers and wrappers.

I saw a few animals called *cucamonde*. Their appearance is like a large rodent, and they scared me. When I would turn in for the night after training, I made sure that there was no way they could get into my tent. The mosquitoes were eating me alive; they must have thrived on our disgusting scents because we smelled worse than toilet water, not being able to bathe for about a week at a time.

Despite the extreme heat and humidity, we couldn't remove any of our clothing because of those little blood suckers. It was absolute torture; warfare in the jungle environment is very rough. I can't say that I know what the soldiers in Vietnam went through, but the jungle itself was a formidable adversary. For me, the jungle was a strange experience; I often heard little footsteps and whispering. My life in the miserably hot jungles of Panama was nearly unbearable.

Once, when I was out walking with the rest of my squadron, we came into an open field. There were no trees in sight, yet I ran into what felt like a wall of cobwebs. I reached up to use my hand to wipe it off my face, but there was nothing there. My crown chakra began to tingle and I sensed anger around me. Being psychic can really be very confusing to someone who doesn't realize what is happening. I said nothing about it. I simply walked on as though nothing had occurred. I didn't know if they were feeling what I was feeling, and I didn't want the other soldiers to think that I was weird, or worse.

The sensation of anger I was feeling in the energy around me had a definite message, and I realized that we were intruding. We were not wanted there. It was as if we were trespassing in a field where we didn't belong.

Today, through study, I know the nature of the presence there and who those spiritual creatures were. In ancient writings they are called "elementals." An elemental first appeared as a mythological being in the alchemical works of Paracelsus, a highly respected physician, who was also a genius in the alchemy and astrology arena in the 16th century. Elementals are mythic beings that can consist of gnomes, undines, sylphs, and fairies, just to name a few.

The basic concept of an elemental refers to the ancient idea of the elements (fire, earth, air and water) as fundamental building blocks of Nature. Each of the four types of elementals, referenced in traditional alchemy writing, influences one of each of the four elements: Gnomes are earth elementals; undines, also known as nymphs, are water elementals; sylphs are air elementals, and salamanders are fire elementals. The exact term for each type varies somewhat from source to source, though these four are now the most common.

Most of these beings are found in folklore as well as in alchemy; their names are often used interchangeably with similar beings from folklore. The sylph, however, is rarely encountered outside of alchemical contexts and fan media. To this day, some people still believe in elementals – those claiming to work in witchcraft and other beliefs systems centered in the natural world. This paradigm was highly influential in medieval natural philosophy, and Paracelsus evidently intended to draw a range of mythological beings into this paradigm by identifying them as belonging to one of these four elemental types.

The training month in Panama was over and we all graduated as Jungle Experts. I was given my patch and a certificate. The patch was fixed to all my fatigues and uniforms for display, but to be honest, one month out in the jungle doesn't really make you a jungle expert. Perhaps, if I were stationed in a base for two years surrounded by jungles to train in, then I could truly consider myself a jungle expert.

I was happy to leave the jungle behind and head back to the cooling rains of the Northwest. When I got back to Fort Lewis, I was focused on finding another stepping stone toward my goal. I still needed some points to be considered for a promotion. So, I decided to sign up for *Cold Weather*

Training in Alaska. While I waited for the next training venture to begin, I continued to show myself to be a serious soldier. That is what I signed up to be and I did hope that my superior officers would notice my diligence. When my orders came in, I had mixed feelings about it. I knew it was going to be freezing, but I was excited to get started on my next adventure. I was impressed with my own daring; I went from the hot jungles of Panama to the icy coldness of Alaskan glaciers.

The Northern Warfare Training Center (NWTC) is a U.S. Army installation located in Black Rapids, Alaska. It was the Army's only cold region training component at the time.

Our airplane landed in Anchorage, where we were picked up by the Army version of the "horse truck" we had traveled in during Basic Training. There were so many soldiers there that we filled up 10 of those trucks. We received a briefing; after that, we were issued our cold weather gear.

The barracks were larger than most I had stayed in. It was one building where all of the soldiers stayed when we weren't out in the field training. While there, I had two roommates. We only slept there, though; we didn't stay in the barracks during our off time. We had two days before our departure, so we went to the non-commissioned officers club, where we mostly drank and listened to music and played pool. After those first two days, we were off to our destination: the glaciers.

We were divided into squads of twelve. They assigned one squad leader who was a staff sergeant on my squad. I was a corporal at the time, so I didn't have the rank for that position. We were instructed on how to care for and put on our skis. A short class was given on cross-country skiing. We had sleighs that were packed with our equipment. Several of

62

us had to push a sleigh cross-country style to the campsite. Since it was my first time doing this, I was utterly exhausted by the end. The whole way there, all I could think was: *When are we going to get there already?*

When we arrived at the campsite, each squad was assigned an area where we unpacked our sleigh and erected our squad team's 12-man tent. Each tent had its own Yukon stove, which would be placed in the middle of the tent so the heat would be distributed evenly. The women soldiers shared their own tent.

We started our two weeks in Cold Weather Combat Training learning some basic skiing; I didn't think two weeks was enough. I had never skied before, and I have to admit it was a lot of fun. I used to crash and fall all the time; I hit a tree once! I walked away unscathed. We spent the whole two weeks skiing, tumbling, and getting up again. We had our rucksacks strapped on our backs, and our M-16s at the ready. It wasn't easy getting around with our cold-weather boots on at all times. If we didn't have them on, though, we would get frostbite.

One night after chow, we were preparing to turn in. The Yukon stove in the center of the tent was on, as the already freezing temperatures were expected to continue plummeting during the night. We had laid all twelve sleeping bags out in a circle along the inner perimeter of the round tent. All of a sudden, I felt strange — ill. I didn't understand it because I had felt great all day. While I was lying there, a soldier to my right went to the squad leader and complained that he wasn't feeling well. To my surprise, after the other soldier was taken to the medic, I began to feel better. The ill feeling had completely gone away. My empathic sensibilities had attached the other soldier's discomfort to me. I didn't know anything at that time about how to ground, center, and shield myself, and even now, that doesn't always protect me when energies are coming in heavy form from all different directions.

We stayed near the glaciers for two weeks. It was 60 degrees below zero when we got up for morning chow. Some of the guys didn't handle the stress of the icy conditions well. Personally I am a cold-weather person. I've always avoided the states where it's hot; I prefer winter to summertime. Nevertheless, Alaska was even too cold for *me* and is at the top of the list of places I will never consider living. I prefer the winters of New York.

While I was in Alaska, I didn't have the time to go sightseeing. I was there just for the cold-weather training. But while training out in the field, next to the glaciers, I was able to enjoy the glistening white of the mountains around me. The air was very clean and brisk. I didn't feel anything paranormal there; it was so clear that my chakras weren't activating at all. The only incident of that kind was the one when I felt ill in the tent when I was near the ill soldier.

The two weeks were soon over, and it was time to pack up and head back to the barracks. Our fun on the slopes had come to an end; our morning chow in 60 degrees below would not be missed. We were so happy that it was over – everyone was going back with all their toes! I graduated from Cold Weather Training with another good report, and another notch was entered into my record; I was one class closer to the change in rank I was working toward.

Back at Fort Lewis, we quickly resumed our daily routines. Soon after our return, the company commander came, with the company first sergeant, to the front of our morning formation. He was carrying a piece of paper, a list of names. When I heard them call out: "Corporal Freddie Rivera, up-front!" I double-timed, which means I ran at a moderate pace.

There were four of us standing in front of the whole company. When he got to me, the First Sergeant said "Corporal Freddie Rivera, you are now promoted to the rank of Sergeant E-5." He uttered many more words, but I don't remember them. I was ecstatic and nervous with anticipation. The captain removed my corporal rank from my lapels, and replaced them with the three stripes of Sergeant E-5, also known as "Buck Sergeant."

As a sergeant, I was given my own squad of twelve soldiers to lead. It wasn't easy. Each of those individuals had joined the Army for reasons that were as varied as they were themselves. Let's just say I didn't have the cream of the crop. Some of those soldiers drank to excess, barely followed orders, or had other problems; they often did the minimum asked of them. With a bit of luck and for whatever reason, I kept up with them. I knew them all very well, not to say that I was buddy-buddy with all of them; I just knew things about them — I felt it. My psychic abilities gave me an advantage that neither they nor I knew that I had. I followed what I felt, and most of the time it worked to my and the Army's advantage. It wasn't the sternest squad, but I managed to keep them on track and in line.

The Army, for me, was a sea of empathy. I always felt like a human sponge, assimilating all of the other soldiers' feelings. I tapped into it all. At this time, of course, I still didn't know that I was psychic. I also knew nothing about what grounding, centering, and shielding myself was; I was completely, unknowingly, leaving myself out in the open.

My reason for joining the Army was to save money and be eligible for the G-I Bill. I didn't have any intention of making a career out of the military. That is what they call a lifer, and that I was *definitely not*. I did not reenlist; my stint in the Army ended in 1983. The Army was a very good experience for me. I learned how to deal with people; I can honestly say that I grew up in the Army. It was hard, but I found out that if I could do that, and because I did, I could do just about anything.

Chapter Three
Leaving My Body

"The intuitive mind is a *sacred gift* and the rational mind is a faithful servant. We have created a society that honors the servant and has *forgotten the gift.* We will not solve the problems of the world from the same level of thinking we were at when we created them. More than anything else, this new century demands new thinking; we must change our materially based analyses of the world around us to include broader, more *multidimensional* perspectives." - *Albert Einstein*

In June of 2008, I was lying in bed when I heard a vibrating, clanging sound. As soon as it began, I knew what was coming next. The first time this happened, I was ten years old. In those initial moments, as I tightened, waiting for the unknown, I felt my senses heighten. I became aware of everything that was going on around me all at one time. Since then, I have taught myself to relax and just let it happen. As I ease myself into a relaxed state, I feel myself rising up from my body. This is not about my *physical body* that lay there very still, but it is my astral counterpart. I am having an *Out-Of-Body-Experience* (OOBE).

This phenomenon occurs naturally and unexpectedly; it changes as one becomes more experienced. In my case, it started when I was a child and I was very afraid when it happened. But as my astral experiences became considerably more frequent, my skills strengthened and I developed more control. I became bolder after some time and, as bedtime approached, I became anxious to start another astral journey.

One day after my first experiences as a child, I was compelled to turn the TV on. As I flipped through the channels, I paused on a documentary that was describing the experiences I had been having. I realize now that a spirit guide may have been directing me; the show had to do with different kinds of paranormal phenomena. They were exploring a range of different experiences that were all too familiar to me. I quickly tried to silence everyone; a few of my cousins were over and making a huge ruckus. In the documentary, a woman was describing an experience similar to mine — it was exactly what had been happening to me and it had a name: *Astral Projection.*

While I listened, I felt as though the explanation of my whole world depended on what she was talking about. At only ten years old, I was dumbfounded. I thought, "Wow. I am a super hero. I am Astro Man." I think about that today, and it puts a smile on my face; I actually thought that I had some super power. I didn't realize that millions of people have out-of-body experiences all the time.

I learned that I had to be careful not to move too fast while on my astral journeys or I would snap back into my body. It had already happened to me many times because I would become overly enthusiastic. I willed myself to stand still on the floor; then I started walking around my room at a slow purposeful stride. The atmosphere looked fluorescent, radiant at first, but it soon lost that appearance and the scene became clear. I turned around and saw myself on my bed sleeping; it's a strange feeling looking at oneself that way. I had gained some weight, I noticed, and thought: *I need to take off a few pounds.* Perhaps this thought was generated more by the feeling of weightlessness I experienced in that moment — how wonderful not to have the weight of a physical body holding me down. I was just energy.

There is great exhilaration that comes with having an out-of-body experience. We are not shackled on this earth plane by the physical form. Here, we feel the degradation of the body throughout the years. Our illnesses, aging, the pull of gravity, and everything that affects us as physical beings, are completely gone when we are out of our bodies.

Entering the living room, I walked to the window. I looked out to see the most beautiful sky I had ever seen. Everything looked crisp, the colors more vibrant and different than they appear when we see with our physical eyes. It's like looking at the world in the highest definition. In New York City today, you don't see as many stars as you could have years ago. You might see a couple. Before the smog got really bad, when we looked at the sky, it was full of them. They were very clear and bright. The moon was brilliant. It looked like I could reach up and touch it. If I had wanted to that night, I could have done so. The visual experience was phenomenal. My surroundings didn't look like my neighborhood looks now, at all. Everything looked clean and new; there was no garbage in the streets. The buildings looked like they had just been built.

I began to notice people in the street. These people looked as if they if they knew I was there and they were observing me in return; they sensed me. I had the feeling they weren't physically alive, but that they were spirits in another realm. They knew I was different, I wasn't completely like them. We, as human beings, are spirits housed in a physical body and they could tell the difference — that in some sense, I was still attached to a physical body and they weren't. This is my only coherent explanation of this.

I was feeling a bit nervous and scared that I was unable to enter back into my body. *Relax, Freddie.* I told myself, and I slowly began to return to my body. When I opened my eyes, I couldn't believe the experience I had just had. It was strange, chilling, and exciting all at the same time; it was breathtaking. I wanted to tell someone, but it was three o'clock in the

69

morning. Besides, who would have believed me?

Out-of-body experiences are astonishing. Sometimes, while astral projecting, I would just fly around. I would be able to fly into outer space, "going to places that no man has gone before." I have discovered and visited several astral realms. The higher the realm, the more incredible it is, and the closer you are to God. The astral traveler doesn't have a choice about where they are going. I have an idea that where one goes has to do with how one is feeling before traveling.

Each astral realm has its own vibration, and beings in those realms are matching the vibrational level of the realm they are in. The beings in the lower realms aren't as evolved as those who are in the higher realms. Once, when I wasn't feeling very well, my vibration emanated at a lower level. As I became more educated, I made it a habit to pray, then ground and center before going to bed. This prepared me for astral traveling in case I was to experience it that night. I visualize a white light bubble of protection around me with an armor plate around it. In time, I have learned to control my travels by sleeping on my side. That works most of the time — not to say that I don't have negative experiences occasionally.

Along with astral projection, I began to experience something else during my sleep. I began to experience *lucid dreaming*, also referred to as having a "conscious dream." A lucid dream isn't as clear as astral projecting. It's a dream in which the person is aware that they are dreaming. When the dreamer is lucid, they can actively take part in and manipulate the dream. You become the director of your dream. A conscious dream can be extremely vivid and real, depending on a person's level of self-awareness while experiencing it.

I have found that I can't fly around the environment when lucid dreaming, as I do in astral projection, and it can be a bit unnerving because at times I come in and out of lucidity. I

70

learned a technique, though, to help me remain lucid: I have learned that if I stay in a well-lighted environment, I won't fall into a non-lucid dream state.

From my childhood and into my adult life, I have always been a die-hard Star Trek fan. That would make me a "Star Trekker." I am amazed with the "Holodeck." The Holodeck is depicted as an enclosed room in which objects and people are simulated by a combination of transported matter, replicated matter, tractor beams, and shaped force fields onto which holographic images are projected. The user enters a huge room and chooses a computer program that includes a place and the people in that place. The user actively interacts with the program and its characters. I can't say that is what astral projection is completely like, but it's similar.

I was always a dreamer. I would close my eyes and visualize. My visualization skills are strong, and this is beneficial for strengthening one's clairvoyance. I didn't know as a child that it's a form of meditation. That is why I became a staunch clairvoyant. If you visualize or vividly fantasize all of the time, don't be surprised if you start to know things before they happen. You might start to see little movies or images in your head that you aren't imagining on your own. When you touch an object and you begin to see a variety of impressions; that is called *psychometry*. This is a form of clairsentience. When my out-of-body experiences became less frequent, I became a bit concerned. It had been a part of my life for so long that I wanted to find out why it had changed. I went to the library and picked up several books on astral projection. The authors suggested a sequence of steps to follow to help: eating too late can spoil your chances of success, so I discontinued eating after six in the evening; lying face up with my arms at my side was suggested so I did that as well; I breathed in through my nose and out through my mouth in a slow paced rhythm.

I waited hopefully to hear the vibrating, clanging sound.

The first night, nothing happened; I tried it again the next night and achieved success. First I heard the loud clanging and then a flash occurred. I felt myself floating up and willed myself to stand on the floor when something happened: I was abruptly snapped back into my body. My heart was pounding rapidly and I had to concentrate on relaxing. I was concerned because nothing like this had ever occurred before. It was an unnerving experience and I decided to abandon the idea for the night. I turned over and went to sleep. After that experience, though, it was as if I had been given a much needed jump-start; my natural rhythm of out-of-body experience returned.

Now, at fifty-seven, I find that my astral projection occurs less often than it did when I was younger. Even when following the guidelines to achieve a successful out-of-body experience, I may not have the desired results. If it doesn't happen, I'm not troubled about it nowadays. When I am successful and I return to my body, it's hard for me to fall back to sleep. In the morning, I wake up tired because of it.

It doesn't help that I am a type two diabetic. I suffer from diabetic neuropathy, a common complication in diabetics in which the nerves are damaged, accompanied by high blood sugar levels. This creates a problem when I try to have an out-of-body experience. When my legs are too relaxed, I feel a discomfort in them. This discomfort disrupts my attempts to travel. I am now taking medication to alleviate that.

There is no way that I can bring you entirely into my astral travel experiences, but I hope that by sharing the following journeys with you, you will get a glimpse.

I Traveled through an Astral Wormhole

I often see people who stand in opposition to the ancient mysteries and simply refer to them as myths. These are usually scientists and others who are trained to base their conclusions on physically observable, provable facts. Yet the late Albert Einstein used the ancient process of visualization in which he saw himself riding on the end of a beam of light. From this, he was able to formulate his theory of light and relativity. Think of it, one of the greatest minds of our time was no doubt experiencing *"Astral Projection."* It is apparent that Einstein developed a synergy between material science and myth, including specific skills that are taught in many mystery traditions.

During one of my spontaneous astral travels, I left my body and willed myself to stand on the floor. I walked into my living room toward a small bench when, unexpectedly, I felt a force take me; I just let it happen. I slipped into what is called an *astral wormhole*. To give you a visual reference, if you have ever seen *Stargate SG1* (A Canadian-American adventure and military science fiction television series), you will know what a wormhole is: it's a tunnel that connects one end of space to another or a specific location. You can travel cosmic distances in a very short time. A trip that would take a spaceship one whole year to reach its destination would take only a matter of seconds when traveling through a wormhole. I did some research on the Internet for astral wormholes, and to my amazement, other astral travelers have shared this same experience.

As I was flying at an extraordinary speed through this wormhole, I noticed that its walls appeared metallic. It also had a silvery pattern to it. It was so breathtaking and exciting that I was astounded. I didn't snap back into my body this time. At the end of this joyride, and on the other side, my exit

73

from the wormhole was below the bluest water I have ever seen. It was alarming and fantastic; I was under water, but I wasn't drowning because I was in astral form. I swam up to the surface.

Once I was above water, I looked around and saw what appeared to be a wooden pier or dock. At its end, I saw an unusual looking being. Its large, shaggy appearance brought the legendary big foot creature to my mind. I thought I saw a sort of smile on its face. I felt it was a sentient being and I sensed it was friendly. I swam to the sandy shore and to my astonishment saw all kinds of beings, apparently from other astral planes or planets.

I observed them and tried to survey them with my eyes and with my own perception. That might have appeared a bit rude of me, but I couldn't help it. It was the same as being on a beach on Earth and watching people converse, enjoying themselves. I realized that I was in an astral galaxy, an intergalactic one. A few beings looked human to me, but no one seemed to pay me any interest, they just walked by me. I guess they are used to astral travelers dropping in.

I have read that from 15 to 20 percent of the Earth's population have had an out-of-body experience in their lifetime. This percentage means that millions of people have this in common. The beings I encountered on this journey weren't surprised to see me there at all. It must be very common for an astral traveler to spontaneously appear, so it was not something that should take them by surprise. I wondered which ones were also astral travelers and which ones were spirits; then I realized that when I am not in my body, I am also a spirit. Like them, I am pure energy.

I became so excited that I came back to my physical body. I tried to return to the astral plane, but I couldn't. I could not forget nor shake the feeling of enthusiasm over the experience I had just had; I could only smile and bask in the wonder of it. Amused, I sat down and wrote it all in my journal, hoping one day to return there again.

Was It or Wasn't It Louise?

One evening, I had a particularly interesting experience. I had lain down flat with one pillow. If I prop my head up too high, it will hinder my chances of having a successful out-of-body experience. I closed my eyes and placed my arms to my sides, palms down. It took me a while to relax because I'd had a hectic day. I found it hard to keep focus, and my mind kept drifting off to other things.

At last, I began to relax and went into a light meditation. My visualization was, *I am an eagle soaring through the clear blue sky, green meadows, and pristine rivers.*

I soon heard that familiar loud clanging sound and arose from my body. Willing myself to stand on the floor and walk to the living room, I approached the window. I decided to take flight. I jumped out of the window and began to fly around. It was an amazing feeling.

After a while, I decided to land where there were many people walking around. The street reminded me of Greenwich Village in New York City. There were restaurants, stores, and art galleries. I felt like I wanted to converse with everyone. I saw a tavern and decided to go inside. There were about eight people inside who were standing around talking. Some were just staring at each other, as if they were telepathically communicating.

I began speaking to a woman, but then I started to feel as though I were going to go back to my body. I concentrated and I remained there; however, everything in the scene changed. The people were sitting down eating this time, and the woman was gone.

Beings don't need to eat in these astral realms, of course, because they are composed of energy. Some spirits in these realms mimic what they did when they were physical beings. They are not biological beings, but some may pretend to still eat food, smoke or drink. This gives them the sensation of what they experienced and relished while in physical form. I saw goodies and refreshments and asked if I could have a slice of cake. I was curious to see if I could taste anything. Someone telepathically said to me, "Yes, in the refrigerator you can find a piece." I said thank you with my mouth, but I wasn't directing it to anyone in particular; I didn't know who spoke to me. I took out a small piece of chocolate cake, my favorite, and I took a bite. I realized that what I *tasted* was just a memory of what chocolate tastes like in physical life, a very faded memory.

I started to feel as though I were going back to my body. I again concentrated and was able to stay. This time, I was standing in a room with just a couple of people. I had a lot of questions to ask my spirit guides. I thought of one in particular. Louise is my mediumship development guide. There are others that I communicate with, but Louise is the one that I converse with the most.

I called out *"Louise, please come to me!"* I waited for a little while, then I called out again. A cat that looked like one I had had as a child, named Goldie, suddenly appeared and started coming toward me; she stopped just in front of me. I asked the cat *"Are you Louise, my spirit guide?"* I asked because I knew that spirits can take on any shape they want to; they are all shape-shifters.

The cat telepathically said "Yes, this is Louise." I was overjoyed! Louise stands by me when I am giving readings. She gives me information about the sitter. If there is more than one spirit that wants to communicate with the sitter, she will organize them. She will do this task so that they won't all try to communicate with me at the same time. This also makes Louise a gatekeeper spirit guide. Sometimes, it doesn't go this way at all; some spirits can be aggressive and want to be heard right away.

I want to express, though, that I didn't know if the spirit was truly Louise or not. This is because I had a feeling of uneasiness. I felt that because I wanted to communicate with Louise so badly, I may have created the encounter myself.

Suddenly, the cat turned into a young woman about the age of twenty-five. She began to talk to another woman in the room. I stood there looking and listening to them, but I couldn't make out what they were saying. I lost control and came back to my body. Later, I asked Louise if she was the one I saw while I was astral projecting and she said "No, it was not me." The entity that I had encountered wasn't a negative one, though. I was in a realm of higher vibration, and lower vibrational entities can't exist there. I feel that I must have reverted to a sleep state and I didn't realize it. What transpired couldn't have happened while I was still astral projecting; next time I will be more careful.

A Trip to I Don't Know Where!

I had been having difficulty getting a restful night's sleep. My ability to have out-of-body experiences was affected. This was before I was diagnosed with the neuropathy, so I wasn't taking any medication for it yet. I researched the Internet about how to get a restful sleep. I was happy because I found things I could do. For instance, staring at a television or computer monitor for a lengthy period during the evening can hinder your chances of falling asleep right away. Monitors send signals to your brain that inhibit sleep. I hadn't known this. I also learned of foods and liquids that promote sleep. A cup of chamomile tea calms the nerves and encourages sleep. That night I turned off my television and computer two hours before I went to bed. I had a cup of the tea and read until midnight (which is usually the time I go to bed). I fell asleep almost immediately. I slept the whole night, and I wasn't bothered by my neuropathy.

That Friday night I went to bed with the hope that I would have an out-of-body experience, but I didn't. I couldn't sleep, so I got up at about 5 a.m., made myself a cup of coffee and sat down to read. About two hours later, I decided to go back to bed. I hoped to get another hour of sleep. I seemed ready to have an out-of-body experience right away, yet I was having a hard time actually leaving my body. I came back to myself and noticed that I had my arm across my face. This was the reason I couldn't get out. I had learned about this possible hindrance from my reading about out-of-body experiences. It happened to me on another occasion as well, when I had one of my legs crossed over the other.

I placed my arms to my sides, palms down. I began to relax and lightly meditate. The neuropathy wasn't bothering me; I began to astral project again. This time, I mentally willed myself to float up and then to stand on the floor. It was a bit emotional for me because I hadn't had an out-of-body experience in about three months, due to my condition. Having begun to practice out-of-body experiences from the age of ten years old had made it an integral part of my life. I felt like I was missing a limb — I wasn't myself.

I have mentioned the lower levels before. When I do end up in one of these lower levels, which is where the less evolved entities reside, I always meet the strangest characters. I never stay there very long and I come back to my body. Sometimes the people I see during astral travel are very busy working, selling food and other items.

During that particular out-of-body experience, I emerged into a beautiful sunny day. I was flying around, feeling very grateful to have this experience back again. I decided to land on a busy street when I noticed that I wasn't wearing any pants. I was in my underwear, which is all I sleep in sometimes. I felt embarrassed and laughed a nervous laugh, and then I walked into a shop and asked if I could have a pair of pants. They obliged me and I quickly put them on. As I started to walk around, I recognized that I was on a higher astral plane. Thank God! After not having had an out-of-body experience for the past three months, I was pleased that I hadn't ended up at a lower level.

It was a beautiful city, clean and modern. I didn't talk to anyone. I sometimes avoid talking to people I meet while astral traveling because communication can be a bit confusing. They might or might not have responded to me if I had tried to start a conversation. They knew I was an astral traveler, and I can just imagine the problems they'd had with physical beings that visit their realms in astral form.

I was sightseeing and at one point, I looked upward and saw a city in the sky. It was far above me and in the clouds; it was just floating. I decided to fly there, but I couldn't take flight because I was starting to *"chime out"* (come back to my physical body). It was because of the neuropathy; it was starting to act up and cause discomfort in my legs. I couldn't focus anymore; I slowly came back to my physical body.

Prior to reentering my body, I heard singing. It was a beautiful female voice accompanied by music. She sounded a bit like Barbra Streisand, but it was not her. If I knew about music, how to write it just by hearing it, I would gladly have noted this melody down. Perhaps I would be perceived as a musical genius today. I wonder if we have heard and then composed music here on Earth that originated from the astral planes. I am sure we have. It is not a surprising concept to realize that some musical artists have astral projected and gained musical inspiration. An interesting volume on this subject is *Unfinished Symphonies* by Rosemary Brown.

Go Tell It on the Mountain

I want to share an experience that has meant a great deal to me. I never doubted it before, but now I *know* that there is a God, and a place that many call Heaven.

One day I was lying down on the couch when I began to go into an astral trance. What I mean by an astral trance is that I step into the spirit dimension without any intention to do so. I don't know how to explain it, but it's like instantly phasing into the spirit dimension. I don't hear the loud clanging, and I don't feel myself rising up from my body, and it's not a lucid dream.

Instantly I found myself standing in a street that was filled with people. It was a beautiful sunny day in what appeared to be a big city. I caught sight of two nuns; they smiled lovingly at me. I heard a chorus singing *Go Tell It on the Mountain*, compiled in the 1800s by John Wesley Work, Jr. It was so beautiful, I am sure it was sung by angels.

I came out of the trance feeling enlightened and emotional; I felt that the nuns had wanted me to hear that music. I looked around and listened, there wasn't any music playing. There was no radio or television on. The windows were closed, yet the sound had been so clear and loud that it couldn't have come from any place other than the apartment. I was hearing it with my *inner ear*, not with my physical ones. The two nuns I'd seen in the astral realm were looking and smiling at me for a reason; maybe they knew that I was going to receive the musical gift of that composition.

I was extremely moved and I needed to tell someone. I must have sounded excited when I called my friend. She asked me *"Freddie*, what is wrong with you?" I told her all about my experience. She is a sensitive herself, and she wasn't at all surprised. Later that same day, I went on the Internet and found the song on YouTube. I played it repeatedly. I thanked God, Jesus, the Angels, and my Spirit Guides for making me feel so special and giving me that gift. The rendition I heard in the astral realm was exceedingly beautiful. It is an experience that will remain embedded in my heart always.

Being clairaudient can truly be a beautiful gift. I hear singing and music all the time from the higher astral realms. I have to confess that there are two sides to it, though: sometimes I hear spirits that might be considered negative as well. Sometimes they may curse, manifest hostile touching, threaten, or suggest bad behavior. I feel that God has given me my abilities to help those that are being provoked by negative energies. A person must accept that the good and the bad come hand in hand.

The Boy in the Mirror

Along with many others, as I mentioned in Chapter 2, I view reincarnation as a fact. After shedding one physical body, we come back to this Earth plane to learn more lessons. We come back because we choose to. The more we learn, the higher we evolve on the other side, and the closer we get to God.

When a lifetime here is completed, we join our soul groups on the Other Side where we review and develop the understanding acquired on the earth plane. After a time, we will live a physical life again. In our physical bodies, we continue to learn and evolve spiritually. We choose this cyclical course.

Most astral travels are very short. I have to say that the longest out-of-body experience I have had was about ten minutes long. I have heard of others traveling for an hour or more. To me, that's astonishing.

My usual routine is to get up very early in the morning to write (about 5 a.m.). I do this because everything is quiet.

One morning in April 2011, I went back to bed at 6:30 a.m. after writing for almost two hours. I experienced a short period of astral travel. I had to write about it because it was the first time I have had this kind of experience. As I left my body, I willed myself to stand on the floor. I knew that once I came back to my body, I would wake up. I didn't want that; I needed more sleep. I stayed in my astral body and walked around the apartment. In the bathroom I looked into the mirror. There was someone looking back at me. He was about seventeen or eighteen years old, had curly blond hair and blue eyes. He was mimicking my every move, just like a reflection in the mirror. I wondered who he was. I leaned my face nearer to the mirror and so did he. I wanted to examine him to see who he was. I came back to myself and opened my eyes. I thought, *Was that me in another life?* but I was confused about that idea.

I was born in 1957, and the boy in the mirror looked too contemporary to be me. He didn't appear to be like someone from the past. He was wearing a T-shirt and jeans. The way he wore his hair was too modern as well. I had never seen this boy before, but his eyes looked a bit similar to mine.

I also wondered, *Are we able to see who we are going to be in a future life?*

Clairvoyants can have a glimpse into the future. I have proven this many times, giving sitters information about events that haven't happened yet, and then they come to pass. This out-of-body experience might have let me see beyond time and space. I feel that it's a mixture of clairvoyance and astral projection. I have a feeling that my questions will be answered concerning this boy someday. It might have been a future premonition of someone I am going to run into, and it might have some significance in my life. I shall see.

A Trip to the Lower Realms Over and Over Again

I found that when I would go to a certain realm I hadn't been feeling well. This type of out-of-body experience I truly hated; it didn't just happen once, but several times. The neuropathy would make me jittery and uncomfortable while trying to fall asleep. It would make my vibration lower. Now, I take medication that controls it; I don't know what I would do without it.

These particular travels start out differently. I don't hear the loud vibrational clanging, and I don't experience the knowing that I am going to have an out-of-body experience; so I can't prepare myself for it.

Normally, when it starts out, I feel my crown and third-eye chakras going crazy. The crown chakra is located on the top of the head, and the third-eye chakra is located between, and just above, the eyebrows. The third-eye chakra is also known as the "inner eye" and gives us another perspective. The crown chakra is a level of higher consciousness. When these two chakras are activated, it indicates a heavy spiritual presence around me. It's like an alarm system for me. On this occasion I opened my eyes, not realizing that I was actually opening my *astral body* eyes instead of my physical eyes.

There was a black man standing by my bed, to the right of me. I felt he was African-American. I thought, *Is he one of my spirit guides?* When I asked him, he said, *No, I am not.* At least he was honest; there are a lot of spirit tricksters that may pretend that they are spirit guides.

I stood up and he was standing there staring at me. He said, *Hello, Freddie.* I asked him his name and what he wanted, but he didn't answer. He began to walk and the scene changed. I followed him to see where he was going. The spirit realm we were viewing was gray-looking, and it was dirty; the buildings looked like unkempt city tenements.

It turns out that I was going through one of my astral trances. This is how I can best describe it. It happens when I am lying down and I am about to fall asleep. I start to transition into the spirit realm and my crown and third-eye chakras start to spin very quickly. The energy is so heavy and powerful that when this happens, I know there are spirits present.

I didn't feel that this man could, or would, harm me in any way. I did feel that he wanted something from me. I asked for guidance from my spirit guides and I finally understood that he was asking for help. The last time I saw him, I asked him *What is it you want from me?* and I noticed that he looked up when I asked that question. Then it dawned on me he wanted to move up to the higher realms and he needed help in doing so.

I saw other spirits in the streets as well, and they all felt the same to me. It was not the way they appeared by description, but by *reason*. There were all kinds of people there: white, black, Hispanic, Asian, you name it. They say that like attracts like, and I sensed that the spirits in this realm were all there for the same reasons. They hadn't been very nice when they were physical beings. I didn't feel as though they were murderers or anything like that, just that they had lived very hard or abusive lives. These were thieves, drug addicts, and severe alcoholics. They were kept back in this realm because during their lives they treated people badly and brought bad karma on themselves. I didn't like going to this place. I learned that when I wasn't feeling well, my vibration was lower and therefore I was more vulnerable to them.

Many of the spirits that reside in that realm do need help. They know there is a better place, and they are willing to transform their behaviors to get there. They need assistance in cleansing their bad karma to get to a higher level, and keep evolving so they can keep moving up.

I recognized what it was that I needed to do. The man who had come to me, wanted me to pray for him and those poor souls in that realm. I have never been a religious person, but I am a spiritual one. I know there is a God and Jesus Christ is my ascended brother. I consider myself a Spiritualist Christian. I have found that the capacity of prayer is powerful. I began to pray every night to God and Jesus, asking them to help those unfortunate souls in that realm. Once I began to pray for them, the black man never came back to me again. He never told me his name, but I held his image in my mind while I prayed. I guess that was enough. At least I hope it was.

Astral Alien Travelers

It would be ridiculous to think that we are the only beings that exist in this vast universe. I know that there are other

85

beings. Some possess knowledge and far more advanced psychic abilities than our own. They use what we earthlings have forgotten about long ago. Our true psychic nature is a gift from God and our birthright.

It seems that other beings from other planets and galaxies did not turn away from who they really are; they aren't afraid of who they really are. This has made them more advanced than the human race. They have evolved far more than we have in their spirituality, their metaphysics, science, and technology. It is truly mind-boggling how we could lose so much of who we are.

Throughout their years of evolution, other living beings have mastered their psychic abilities to the point that they don't even have to use their mouths to speak; all communication is done telepathically. This is only one aspect of what they can do.

We are being visited here on Earth not only by UFO's but by astral traveling entities. Some of these cultures have mastered the ability to use their astral bodies to travel to other planets. They do it in groups, or even individually, to study other places throughout the universe. They have exceptional control of their astral bodies. In this form, they can medically examine their own kind and other beings from other planets. They have developed extraordinary healing abilities while in their physical or astral bodies; but when they are in their astral form, they are further advanced. Communicating with spirits is as natural to them as communicating with each other is to us.

One afternoon around 1 p.m., I was napping on the couch. I was facing up with my arms to my sides and I began to go into one of my semi-astral trances. I began to feel the presence of several entities and I noticed that my crown and third-eye chakras weren't going crazy the way they normally do — these entities were different.

I was drawn out of my body about five inches or less. I turned my astral body head to my right, and I saw three figures. I couldn't make them out and I found this confusing. It seemed as though they really didn't want to be seen completely. The room was bright with sunshine, and I still couldn't make them out. They looked like dark silhouettes to me; I could not view them in detail. I didn't feel threatened in any way. I was being coaxed telepathically into feeling calm; I was reassured that they weren't there to harm me.

The smallest entity parted from the other two and approached my physical body, which was still lying on the couch face up. The entity was female and she was standing just behind me. I became aware of two small hands on my head. I reached up quickly and grabbed her left hand with my left astral hand. I startled her, but reassured her that I wasn't going to harm her, by kissing her left hand. She was baffled as to why I would do that; she was equally amazed that I knew she was there. One of the two male entities enlightened her. *He is psychic.* I don't know how or why I understood what he said, but I did. They continued talking, but this time I could not hear them or, they were not *letting* me hear them. I feel that the first time, when I did hear them, must have been by accident. The female entity was doing something to me, examining me. However, I didn't feel any kind of discomfort, just her tender touch. Suddenly she stopped what she was doing and walked to where the other two were.

I kept looking in their direction; then they began to walk away, they just faded out. The whole experience couldn't have lasted more than ten minutes.

I phased back into my body and came out of the astral

dimensional shift. I thought to myself that this was a very different and strange experience. Who were those entities? I wondered. They were in the astral dimension, so that told me that they were in their astral bodies. They were not spirits from the astral realms but, like me, they were astral travelers. Their silhouettes had a human kind of shape to them, but since I couldn't fully see them, I can't give a detailed description. The only thing that I could really distinguish was that they were wearing some type of uniform. After I re-entered my physical body, I contemplated how unique this experience had been.

I thought of the studies that have been done regarding *Star Children*. These children have been sent here from all areas of the Universe. They have been given special assignments to assist people who are in rebirth to raise our planet to higher levels of spiritual consciousness. They possess psychic, spiritual, and other extrasensory abilities. These children will help bring about peace, collapse corrupt systems, and change the direction of dimensional consciousness in the years to come.

I wondered and I wondered some more. *What if they come back?* I wanted to know more. I wanted answers. I contemplated, *How can I get them to answer my questions if they do come back? Furthermore, if they come back, and I don't detect them the way I did before, I won't be able to communicate with them.* I thought of how many other times they may have come to me and I was unaware of them. I know this is a bit of a stretch, but the recognition of it all really had me thinking.

I decided I would become a little radical the next time they come, if they do. I want to ask them why they are here, and why they chose me to come to.

Those entities came to me for a reason. I don't yet know

88

what that reason could be, but I am confident that all will be clear one day.

Chapter Four
El Diablo Empuja

Spirit: (spir . it), A supernatural, incorporeal, rational being or personality, usually regarded as imperceptible at ordinary times to the human senses, but capable of becoming visible at pleasure, and frequently conceived as troublesome, terrifying, or hostile to mankind. — *The Oxford English Dictionary*

Throughout my life, I have heard my mother and others say, "El diablo empuja" (The devil pushes). My mother always made this statement when she became concerned that I could injure myself doing something she considered dangerous. I would reassure her that I would be okay, and then she would say, *"El diablo empuja, tenga culdado!"* (The devil pushes, be careful!). Today, that is more than just a phrase to me, it is a fact; evil does try to harm.

Everything has duality: a positive and a negative. There are the opposites: white and black; up and down; forwards and backwards; and so on. There is an opposing force in everything. If there is good, of course there is evil. I am speaking in the spiritual sense. There are lower-vibrational entities; these entities reside at the very bottom of the astral realms. They are bent on destroying humanity. Many call this lower-level the *underworld*. It's the first realm; it is at the bottom. The higher we advance on the astral levels, the closer we are to God.

In the study of both mythology and religion, the underworld is a generic term for what some call the afterlife. It is referring to any place newly departed souls go. In most cultures, the

91

term refers to a neutral or dystrophic realm of afterlife instead of a heavenly or paradisiacal one. Sometimes the underworld is called *hell*: the abyss that is thought to be under the Earth. This is the realm where Lucifer rules with his minions of demons. These are evil entities that never lived a physical life; they are purely malevolent. However, there are also evil earthbound spirits that were not good people in physical life. They remain earthbound because they are afraid that if they go into the light they will be judged – and deservedly so.

I have experienced hideous crimes in my life; 9/11 was one. I have read of horrible atrocities that human beings have committed against other innocent beings throughout history. It just doesn't register for me how humans can commit those horrific crimes unless they were influenced by evil. For example, the Nazi party grew out of several occult groups that sprung up in the late 19th century as a reaction to the advanced materialism and technology of that era. These groups spoke of the coming of a new Messiah who would save Germany. Young Adolf Hitler took advantage of that restlessness to develop the notion that perhaps he was the chosen one to save the German people.

I don't feel that Hitler developed that notion on his own. I think that the idea was planted in his head by unseen forces, evil forces. If a person already has a dark soul (which Hitler clearly had), it is very easy for that person to be influenced by evil forces. There is a saying that we each walk with a little angel on one shoulder and a devil on the other; every person has the capacity to do both good and evil. Hitler chose evil. The potential was already in his nature. Evil saw the opportunity and took advantage of it. That resulted in the death of millions of people. The majority of people naturally sway to that little angel; most people are good. God has given us all free will to choose; it is up to us how we choose.

I believe that those who give in to evil will suffer the consequences and end up in that first realm.

Going back to our free will to choose, when I prayed, I never used to include myself in my prayers. I always thought of others, the people I love. I would ask God to take care of them, but I never asked God to take care of *me*. One night, when I had been unsuccessful in my desperate search for work, I began to plead with God: "God I need a job, please help me find a job." This was the first time that I prayed for something for myself; I desperately needed a job. It became evident to me that God was listening.

This was in the year 2000. I had applied for a job at Saint John's University as part of a computer graphics Web design team. The interview went well, but I found out later that they hired another candidate. Two months had passed when I received a phone call from the director of the design team. He asked if I was still looking for employment. Without hesitation, I immediately said yes, trying not to sound too desperate. He said that I would start out as a consultant, but that it would turn into a full-time position. I worked as a consultant for three months, making more money than I had ever made before. As the director assured me, the consultant job did turn into a full-time position: I became the senior graphics designer for the Web team.

While I was still working as a consultant, I asked what had happened to the person they had originally hired for the position. One of my co-workers said "She didn't like the job so she decided to leave." I thought: *She didn't like a wonderful job like this? A job that pays this well and has wonderful benefits?* I didn't think she knew what she was doing. I concluded that I had asked God for a job that I needed and God came through for me. The woman who left the job was either confident that she would find another one, or she already had found one that she liked better. I knew that I was heard; God had directed my path in the right course. The whole thing felt quite bizarre to me.

My World fell Apart

It was a cold day in February of 2002; it had snowed the night before. I was in Queens, contentedly working at my desk. St. John's University was warm enough inside, and yes, I still loved my job. Everyone on the team was working as usual. We were especially upbeat because it was a Thursday. Thursday, for us, was equal to most people's Friday. We didn't have to work the next day. It was about 2:30 p.m. when my co-workers and I noticed that our supervisor, Jeffery, wasn't feeling the end-of-the-work-week elation that the rest of us were. He didn't look happy. Just that quickly the mood change swept over us. I felt something coming; I had a very bad feeling.

At 2:45 p.m. two women from the university human resources came into our office. They asked for our attention and introduced themselves. At their request, we stopped what we were doing to listen to what they had to say: "We are sorry to say that this department has been terminated." At that very moment, my heart sank.

We all looked at each other in utter disbelief. I saw, and shared in, the disappointment that was reflected on all our faces. I became extremely flushed and hot all over. I realized if I didn't slow my adrenals down, I was likely to have a panic attack. I felt the concentration of emotional stress and worry from all of my co-workers emanating toward me.

"Please stand and take hold of your belongings and move away from your desk," one of the women firmly instructed. They do this because of their past experience; employees become so angry and distraught that they break things, especially computers. They gave us each a card that had a specified date and time for an appointment with the human resources department and that was pretty much it.

My appointment was for the following Monday. When I got home, I didn't say anything to my mother; I was devastated and still in shock about the unexpected blow. I had no idea what lay ahead. I was about to embark on a path of self-destruction. At that moment, I had no idea what my future held. I was on the brink of the downward spiral that would change my life forever.

Monday took forever to arrive. I kept my appointment and met with the woman who had made the announcement to us. She told me that the university would give me a severance package and that I could also apply for unemployment. She added that I could apply for another position at the university if I so desired. There wasn't anything else that I had experience in doing, so I accepted the package and immediately applied for unemployment benefits.

I felt that finding a job as a graphic artist was going to be extremely difficult. I did apply for jobs, but they were hiring very young graphic designers who were willing to take any pay that was offered to them. This field had become over-crowded; there was too much competition for too few jobs. In the meantime, I fell deeper and deeper into depression; I found myself in a very dark place. For the first two years, between the severance package from the university, unemployment benefits, and the money I had saved up, I did pretty well. But everything was slowly trickling away. I began to drink more, and made myself a larger target for evil.

As a child, I was abused in many ways, but never by my loving mother. Stuttering only exacerbated the traumas that already made my life so very hard to deal with. Being a teenager is always the most difficult time while growing up but, for me, it was nearly intolerable. Everyone thought I was a bit weird and I kept to myself somewhat; my life felt secretive. It was hard to express myself, or even trust anyone. I lived in my own little world. When I got into alcohol, I discovered it allowed me to relax and talk freely; it helped bring me out of my shell.

It's ironic that what killed my father gave me freedom. This freedom eventually spun into a negative dependency that, in the years to come, might have ended my life. As an adult, I didn't stutter as much, even when I was sober; but when I drank, I stuttered even less. In the beginning, the drinking was almost medicinal; as I got older, it all changed. The drinking helped me relax and open up enough to talk to others. It aided me in being able to cope with my psychically sensitive life. Then it began to turn against me.

I was not a daily drinker. I drank only when I thought I needed it. But when I did drink, I drank myself into a stupor. I felt horrible because I could not remember what I did the night before. I have lost a lot, including a few friends, due to the way I vented my anger when intoxicated. I have always looked back with remorse and wished I could go back in time and change things. But, like everyone, I can't change what was. I can only surmise that perhaps these are lessons I had to learn in order to shape me into the person I am today.

My desperate search for work continued without success. I became more and more depressed. I began to have thoughts of suicide and how I should do it. I searched the Internet for information on the best ways to take one's own life. I wanted it to be painless and quick. I wanted no cutting, throwing myself off of a building, drowning, or hanging. I couldn't make up my mind how to go about it. I worried that if it didn't work, I could cripple myself for life. There was a little voice in my head telling me not to do it, but something else pressed me to follow through.

I couldn't talk to anyone about what I was going through. The little voice in my head would encourage me and try to reason with me. "Your mother and family would be heartbroken; you are going to be okay, don't worry. You have a lot of people who will be there in the future to help you." This voice tried to reassure me and let me know that it had come to me on my behalf. Although I was desperate, I knew it wasn't me expressing those thoughts to myself. The voice was clear as day. It was an external message; it would come during the times that I felt numb, times when I needed a break and I didn't want to think anymore. However, I also had evil thoughts that were brutal — a psychic attack — and not only was I not too afraid to commit suicide, but I welcomed the thought. "You're not worth it! Go ahead and take a knife and kill yourself." The feeling was so strong; it wasn't just words. It was a powerful, very frightening, and overwhelming sensation. The evil thoughts were enveloping me. There was a presence lurking and I felt it keenly. It made itself known, revealing itself, and at the same time making me feel as though those thoughts were coming from me.

Some members of my family recognized that there was something wrong with me. They were concerned and questioned me. I just told them that I was fine. But my acute clairsentience was on constant high alert and I couldn't see a way to cope. I never smiled; I just kept to myself. All I wanted was to be left alone. It took a lot out of me when family or friends would come to visit. I would have to be cheery, put on an act that contradicted how I felt inside. I thought I was fooling everybody, but it was obvious to everyone that I was encircled by a dark veil.

One day in February of 2008, I felt a strange sensation, as if I wasn't alone. I had felt a somewhat familiar presence around me before. It wasn't an evil presence. It almost felt like I was surrounded by an unseen group of visitors.

I thought it must be my imagination, so I just let it go.

Later, I had been in bed for about five minutes, when I started to see faces — lots of faces. It was like a slide show. Some were in color, some black and white; some were just outlines of faces. I opened my eyes, bewildered and confused. I sat up on my bed: *What is going on here?* I thought to myself. I lay back down and it began again. This time I allowed the experience to happen. I saw women, men, and children — some smiling, some serious, and some I couldn't make out. It was all happening very fast. While I was watching, I didn't hear anything – no voices, no sound at all. I was mesmerized as I slowly drifted into sleep. That night I didn't have any nightmares at all. It was as though I was sheltered within peace and protection.

I got up early that morning and sat at my computer with my coffee and a cigarette. *Am I going nuts, losing my mind?* I was captivated throughout the day by thoughts about what had happened the previous night. I prayed for God to help me understand; I was afraid I was losing my mind.

I had to be okay. I take care of my mother; she depends on me. *Please don't let this happen to me. Is it a punishment for thinking of suicide? I promise I won't contemplate it again.* I still did not understand that during my days of darkest thoughts, those negative harmful feelings weren't coming from me. *God, with all that has happened to me in my life, I have never lost my faith; please God!*

I sat there in deep thought. My mother asked me, in Spanish:

98

"What is wrong with you? Why are you so quiet?" I didn't want to frighten her, so I didn't tell her about the events of the night before. Instead, I forced myself to snap out of it, and went about doing my chores, my daily routine, as if nothing had happened.

That night, after I readied myself for bed in my usual way and said my prayers, I settled in, ready to relax. It didn't take long before once again the slide show of faces began. I was both astonished and extremely curious about what I was seeing.

I opened and closed my eyes again and again, yet things didn't change. The parade of faces continued from one to the next. Then something new came into the experience. I opened my eyes and caught sight of what looked like a green fluorescent light; it was moving about at the head of the bed.

I looked around to see if the light was coming from somewhere else. The shades were closed, so there was no way a light like that could have come in through the windows. The light moved slowly, as if it had a mind of its own. It wasn't a straight beam of light; it was curvaceous and seemed to want to be noticed. I didn't feel threatened or afraid at all. I felt comforted and at peace and then suddenly sleepy;, as if it was carrying a message to me: "Don't worry, all is well. Now go to sleep." And I did. After that night – my vision of the light, any fear or worry I may have had, was gone. I began to understand intuitively there was a purpose to what was going on; I was soon to find out that feeling was right.

As I prepared for bed the next night, I had no idea that I was about to have a psychic experience that would change my life forever. After I had gone to bed, the faces came in again. I was getting used to their appearance now; I actually expected them. Their presence was comforting. I was always interested in the paranormal, and this was really intriguing.

As I lay there, I got the urge to open my eyes. I turned my face toward the living room, as if I was being directed to look there. I could see a figure slowly materializing; it appeared as if it was squatting down on one knee. The apparition continued to materialize until I could make it out clearly. I wasn't afraid; just as when I had seen the green hue at the bedpost, I was filled with peace.

The figure's physical appearance was that of an East Indian man dressed in white, with a small turban on his head. When I saw him, I thought: *Now it's confirmed, I really am going nuts.* I kept my eyes glued to this apparition; he was transparent, not fully solid. He looked at me and smiled and I realized he was talking to me telepathically; he was conveying to me that he was my Master Spirit Guide and that his name was Andreas.

The term *spirit guide* is usually associated with spiritualist churches. Psychics and mediums define this as a being that chooses to remain discarnate, to enable an incarnated human being to be under their guidance and protection. Usually, these spirit guides have been stereotyped as being Egyptian, Native American, or Chinese – to name a few. These descriptions usually come from spiritualist churches within the western traditions. They seem to support the notion that these are enlightened beings; they are saints and/or beings that come from an ancient wisdom. They have been described as angels, native spirits, animal totems, and others. Today, I know that a *spirit guide* can be just about anyone.

I lay there just staring at him and studying him. I thought maybe I had died and he had come to collect me into the afterlife. At that time, I had never used the term "afterlife." The afterlife means "heaven" to me. The question was, *Is he here to take me to heaven?* Startled at that thought, I was becoming very nervous.

I am not a bad person. I have never intentionally hurt anyone in my life, except for the abuse I inflicted upon myself. *Oh my God*, I thought, *I was only 'thinking' of suicide, but I didn't 'actually' do it, yet.* My nervousness was escalating.

Again, the spirit guide calmed me telepathically; it was so subtle, that I didn't notice immediately.

I realized he was trying to deliver something to me. I became aware that something inside of me was opening up. He was showing me glimpses of myself, the way I was before I shut down. I began to feel the way I did when I was six years old. I have accumulated many gifts since then. I call them "gifts" now because I realized they were given to me by God; I had not always been aware of that.

Human beings are naturally intuitive. Our instincts and intuition are sharpened with use. With development, a person's senses can become greatly amplified, reaching what is referred to as "second level." Psychic abilities at that level are much stronger. Mediumship abilities might come after that. I have read this in biographies of psychics who became mediums later in life. As is often the case, I came into this world with everything "turned on." I am referred to as a "natural medium."

After several minutes of staring at my visitor, I needed a break from the intensity of my thoughts. I decided to assume that I was seeing and hearing things; I turned over and fell asleep. When I got up in the morning, I was still thinking about what had happened: *I have to start taking better care of myself. I can't talk about this to anyone, otherwise they will think I have lost it and label me as crazy.* The thought of madness had become a regular theme in my head for much of my life. I had become aware early in life that not everyone was seeing, hearing, and experiencing the same things I was. I had

101

become used to living this way. Thinking back, I see now that, on this and many other incidents in my life, I was often a bit rude to my special visitors.

I began my morning as though it were any other, shelving all thoughts of the events from the night before. After returning from the kitchen with my coffee, I turned on my computer to check my e-mail. When I glanced into the living room, Andreas was still there, crouching down on one knee with a serene smile.

Oh Lord, what is happening to me? I worried. After a few minutes, I began to feel serene again. I didn't feel that this entity was evil in any way. I can't explain it, I just knew it. Andreas telepathically told me again, *I am your Master Spirit Guide, don't be afraid.* I didn't even know what a master spirit guide was.

I remembered watching Montel Williams when he had Sylvia Brown, a world-renown psychic medium, on the show every Wednesday. She was always talking to audience members about their master or main spirit guides. When I remembered this, I became more interested in what Andreas said about being my Master Spirit Guide. He said, "I am always with you, but am appearing to you now because you are in need, in need of knowing the truth." I was definitely paying attention now, and I asked, "What truth do I need to know?" Andreas didn't answer me and intuitively I knew why — because I needed to find out for myself. He didn't want to influence me. He stayed with me as he continued to give me memories of when I was a little boy. I saw the people and heard the voices from my life before I suffered the trauma that caused me to shut everything out.

I wasn't sure what was happening to me, but I decided to just accept it for the time being; it seemed I had no choice. A week went by while Andreas continued to stay with me; he never left the living room. It was a bit unnerving, seeing him there all the time. I felt like I was under constant surveillance. I wasn't about to start telling people that I was seeing things. I'd held my secrets all this time and I still had my 90-year-old mother to take care of. She was, and still is, my first concern. I was afraid that if I spoke to someone, I would be put away in Bellevue hospital, a well-known psychiatric facility in New York City. I couldn't take that chance. My mother would be left to fend for herself. There was no one else available whom I could trust; I kept my mouth shut for the time being.

I am a Christian and I have come to know that we are never truly alone. In my dilemma, I decided to go out to buy a special candle. I wanted one in the living room with Jesus Christ printed on the glass container; I was thinking that, with the candle and prayers, maybe Andreas would go away.

Walking around my neighborhood, I came across a spiritual store called a "Botanica" — a retail store that sells folk medicine, religious candles, statuary, amulets, and other products regarded as magical, spiritual, or alternative medicine.

I was the only customer in the store; there was a very nice woman behind the counter. She asked me if I needed any help and I told her that I was looking for a candle with Jesus Christ on the glass jar. I mentioned that I lived in the neighborhood and had never noticed this store. She smiled and came from behind the counter and walked me to the aisle where the candles were displayed. I found the one I wanted and told her I would come back again sometime to pick up a few other items.

I left the store and walked to the corner to cross the street. I stopped because I felt a little faint. I thought, *My blood sugar must be getting low.* I was intent on getting home and having something to eat. Before I could even complete the thought, in my mind's eye, I began to see a vision.

I saw the lady in the store with an old lady behind her. The old lady had a serious expression on her face; I felt that she wanted me to come back to the Botanica. Automatically, as if it were the most natural way for me to communicate, I told her telepathically that I would come back in a few days to buy some incense. She became very happy with that response. Her reaction made me smile; she was a very cute little old lady and didn't frighten me at all.

I had never done this before. As a child, I never did what the spirits wanted me to do. I didn't know then that they were spirits. This time I understood there was a purpose. I had seen a famous psychic medium on television many times, and knew that he sees spirits in his mind's eye, hears voices in his head, and is able to communicate telepathically. I remembered the people I had seen in my head as a child, the voices I heard and ignored because I didn't understand what was happening. Now that I grasped that there are people like him, like me, I decided not to ignore it.

For the first time in my life, I embraced my gift of clairaudience and I let it flow; it seemed natural to me. I knew in that moment, I was honoring my true self. It was a step toward my self-acceptance; it felt right.

The vision continued and the little old lady picked up a plate of pancakes! "What is it about the pancakes?" I asked her. No answer; then she put the pancakes down and picked up a bouquet of flowers. She was thanking me and sending me love for being nice to her. I asked her for her name and I saw the letter "M." I quickly spoke the name "Mary," as if she temporarily took control of my mouth and made me say it.

She laughed and nodded her head. "Yes." "Is it Mary?" I enquired. She nodded her head yes again and so, it was Mary. I remember thinking how wonderful it was that my first experience like this was with Mary. "How is the lady in the store related to you?" I asked.

Hearing clairaudiantly is not hearing as one hears a physical being, although, for some reason, I heard Andreas much more clearly. Usually I have to really listen; it comes in pieces and my clairsentience picks up the rest by feelings. Sometimes I have to wait until they shake their heads yes or no, if I can't hear anything by clairaudience.

"Is the woman with you your daughter, a friend, your granddaughter?" I asked. She nodded her head "yes" very fast. "So it's your granddaughter in the store?" I inquired. "Yes," she nodded. "Okay, Mary," I said, "I will be going back to the store in a few days."

All of this occurred while I was still standing at the corner. I wondered if anyone had witnessed me. When I was able to walk on, Mary walked with me for a little while; she continued showing me flowers, thanking me. When I got home, I sat down and I said, "Okay, Mary, you can come back when I am on my way to the store." I said this out loud, using my voice; my mother heard me. She asked, "Why are you talking to yourself?" Mary smiled and her energy faded away. I thought, *Wow, this is incredible!* Mary was gone, but Andreas was still there. He seemed very happy; I wondered why.

On the day when I was ready to go back to the store, Mary suddenly popped into my head. I smiled; she had been eagerly waiting for me. She knew that I would keep my word and, of course, I did.

I walked into the store, realizing that I was very nervous. I knew this had to be done delicately; I had no idea how what I had to say was going to be received. Again, I was the only one in the store, so just to get a conversation started, I asked Mary's granddaughter about incense. After several minutes of general talk, I began the true conversation: "I have something to tell you and, given that you run a store such as this, I think you will be open to it. I hope so, anyway." I said.

"Fine, what is it?" She asked.

I told her what happened when I left the store the other day, and I asked her, "Has your grandmother passed?"

She answered, "Yes, she passed."

I already knew that she had crossed over, of course, but I asked anyway for her sake and just to be sure. "Was her name Mary?" I asked. I saw her expression change; she looked at me with surprise. "Yes, her name was Mary." she said.

"Your grandmother is here with us right now," I said, "and she keeps showing me a plate of pancakes. Do you know why she is holding a plate of pancakes?"

"No." she answered, "I don't know what it means. My grandmother died when I was twelve years old, and I didn't know her that well. She lived far away."

Confirming her grandmother's name gave me a bit of confidence. But here I was bringing forth her grandmother and it seemed to mean nothing to her; I wasn't seeing any kind of reaction to that at all. She didn't seem to have feelings about it. "Your grandmother crossed over from old age; she died peacefully in her sleep." I said.

"Yes, that is what my mother told me," she said.

"She is showing me lots of flowers right now, that indicates that she is saying she loves you." I only knew this because I had heard it mentioned by another medium I had seen. When loved ones want to convey their love, they will show you flowers. In that moment, I was extremely grateful for the opportunity to observe that other medium; if not for that, I may not have known about the significance of the flowers. Now I know that a medium would have to give at least four to five pieces of information, or more, as evidence that it is the person's loved one coming through; that it really is that person.

"Mary is also making me feel that she comes around you a lot. She is showing me that she lays framed pictures face down in your home sometimes."

"Yes," she responded. "I notice pictures in my house that have been laid down that way; I was wondering how they got like that."

"Lots of mediums have told me the same thing." she said. "They only tell me her name and that she is around me; it's not the first time – except for the pancakes, how she died, and the pictures."

So there it was; this was why she wasn't that excited. I laughed and told her that her grandmother was very sweet and a bit funny. She smiled when I shared this. I asked her if she would ask her family about the pancakes; I was curious. She said that she would. I bought my incense and said goodbye. I left with an amazing feeling inside of me. Mary was a very nice person; I felt that she was loved very much by her family.

I am glad that had I watched the other medium on television; it helped me to emulate him. It made what I was doing feel more natural. This experience had come easily, but sometimes it isn't so easy. Sometimes a sitter can get very emotional and start to cry. I have found that I have to remain emotionally detached while giving a reading. If I engage on an emotional level, I will lose the connection. Some have told me that I am very pragmatic and objective. I do try to remain calm; I want the reading to be the sitter's joyful occasion. In my heart, I rejoice with them in the fact that their loved ones aren't really gone.

I went back to the Botanica two days later to buy another candle. The woman behind the counter told me, "I asked my mother about the pancakes and she told me that my grandmother was famous for them." I said, "That is amazing; thank you for that validation."

She asked me, "Do you do private readings? I need someone here to do consultations."

I told her, "I am sorry, but I never asked you for your name." She answered, "It's Darlene." I asked her how she was and said, "My name is Freddie, and I am sorry I didn't ask you for your name before, but I was nervous. I am new at this and you are the first person I have ever delivered a message to from the Other Side. Darlene, I don't do consultations." She looked at me like I was kidding. "Why not, you're so good?" she asked. I understood that she'd had many readings in the past. "That was something that just happened and I took the gamble; I had to see if what was coming to me was real. Thank you, but right now I don't know what I am going to do." She said, "If you ever decide to, please come in and we can talk about it."

I answered, "That is fine Darlene, I will." I paid for my

candle and said goodbye.

When I got home, I looked at Andreas. "I am back," I called out. I did not know at the time that Andreas was with me everywhere I go. I stared at him for a while. Finally I asked "That is why you are here; to let me know that I can do what I did with Mary?" He made me feel like that was part of it, but that wasn't all. He was there for another reason and I would find out soon. I started to recollect what I saw and heard as a child and I said loudly "IT CAME BACK!" The block that had prevented me from recognizing and using my abilities was gone.

Late one evening in March of 2008, I was sitting at my computer. Andreas was with me, squatting on one knee, waiting very patiently. I felt that he was waiting for something that was going to happen. I didn't realize at the time that he was there to offer me his support and to give me strength. As it turned out, something did happen and it was horrifying.

I began to feel strange and I had to stand up. I felt an *energy*, a very different energy than I had felt before. Only as a medium today, do I recognize that the change of energy I felt was my mediumistic abilities awakening within me. They were reawaking, coming back stronger than anything I had ever experienced earlier in my life. I was being flooded with psychic experiences; it seemed that all of my gifts were on high alert. Information was coming to me from every direction. I could see and communicate with spirits in my mind's eye again, as I did as a child. Only now it was with the understanding of an adult. I could feel the barriers that had blocked my awareness of my psychic abilities falling away. I was seeing slideshows of spirits in my mind's eye, and this hit me like a ton of bricks.

As I have mentioned before, there are different types of

mediums. There are mental, spirit, physical, or trance mediums and mediums that can see spirits with their eyes all the time. To me, seeing full-bodied, earthbound spirits walking around all the time would be extremely unnerving. I see spirits in several ways. Sometimes I see part of a shadow-like figure or a transparent mass moving ever so carefully and then fading out, or completely disappearing. These sightings don't last very long, just a few seconds, but I know they are still there. Another way I know that a spirit is present is when I close my eyes and I see round formations with colors; the most common for me is blue. My strongest indication, though, is when my crown and third-eye chakras begin to activate.

While I was standing by my computer, I slowly began to see a creature in my mind's eye. The best way I can describe this creature would be to say that he bears a likeness to the animated character of Gollum in *The Lord of the Rings*. This creature was a bit green in color and nastier looking than anything one would see in a movie. I saw it squatting and moving about on all fours, like a monkey.

The creature was near the front door of the apartment. It quickly became apparent that it realized I could see it, and it became angry. It started to snap at me in my mind's eye, like when a vicious dog is tied up and tries to get to you but can't. It didn't like that I could see and identify it. It seemed to be trying to frighten me into overlooking it, to somehow become unaware of it – as if that were possible! A foul odor assaulted my senses as the creature drew nearer. I looked at Andreas and understood what he was showing me. He was telling me, "Now you see the face of what has been plaguing you."

People who drink alcohol in excess and do drugs, or don't take care of themselves, are very susceptible to these types of

110

evil entities. Their auras are weakened by their lack of self-caring; it's very easy for these entities to attach themselves to them. Bars are just one of the many places where this sort of entity goes to find victims. This particular entity had been with me for a very long time. Under its oppression, I had felt tired, drained, and depressed. I had nightmares and thoughts of suicide, especially after I had been drinking the day before. This creature placed thoughts into my head telepathically, but I was thinking that I was the one who was having those thoughts. It tried to gain full control of me to make me do things – horrible things.

Once I was sitting on the couch when, out of the blue, I started to have thoughts of dread. I saw the entity in my mind's eye, taunting me. I became terrified and I quickly grabbed the Bible my brother Augustine had given me. I started to pray; I prayed like I had never prayed before. I was frozen, sitting there, clutching the Bible to my chest. This was an eye-opening moment for me. I now have a deep realization of how very powerful prayer is. Prayer that comes from the heart, joined by profound faith, is the most powerful. Such faith is something that I am deeply grateful to rely on today.

At times, such as when I was cooking, I would suddenly smell the bad odor and those old dark thoughts would come back into my head. I would have to stand back, breathe deeply, and use the gift of discernment with prayer. This entity was very powerful, but God gave me the strength to fight back and I did. I consider myself a very strong-willed person. This mass of evil was angry, but it couldn't succeed in making me do what it wanted me to do.

I knew it was there, my mother was there with me, too; I didn't want her harmed in any way. It was in this circumstance that I decided to stop drinking; it was hard, but

I did it. My spirit guides and angels knew that I would prevail. They stood back and allowed me to discover myself as the person that they knew I would become. I became a spiritual warrior, using all of the gifts that God gave me. I fought that entity in many ways. Andreas advised me not to talk to it or acknowledge it. I must follow the techniques he had given me to detach from this creature and break free of its hold on my life.

I cleaned the apartment immaculately; this thing had been draining me of my energy for a long time. I hadn't cared much for cleaning the apartment, or even myself; I had gone for weeks without shaving. I bought candles, smudge sage, and I went to war. I lived in constant prayer. I was transforming my surroundings into the kind of environment where this malevolent thing couldn't survive. I was a changed person; a new "Freddie" had emerged. At last the entity departed. I literally *felt* this angry entity leave; it has never returned. If it ever tries it will find that it will get more of the same. Now that I have more experience, it will have no chance at all.

We have to use our free will to invoke the Holy Spirit – and we have to mean it.

God has assigned a team of divine beings to watch over us, but we have to ask for help.

Jesus Christ and my team of spirit guides and angels knew that I would prevail. However, I had to learn some lessons first. I had to change my ways, and get cleaned up.

If you ever feel that evil is around you, stand up and become the *warrior* that I came to be. They only have power over you if you allow it.

When Andreas appeared to me on that first night, it was not only to let me know and show me that my mediumistic abilities had come back. It was to prepare me to defeat the evil that was bent on destroying me. It had very nearly succeeded. It is unable to touch me now. In other words, it was my trust in God together with my mediumship abilities and my willingness to allow the gifts of the spirit to work through me that saved me. Without allowing those gifts to manifest, I would never have known that I had become a target of evil forces.

Chapter Five
Revelations

"Revelation comes on the Lord's
timetable, which often means we must
move forward in faith, even though we
haven't received all the answers
we desire." - *Robert D. Hales*

My belief in spirits began when I was a child. That was when I saw the Grim Reaper and, on another occasion, I saw the frightening unknown ghost in my living room. I saw them with my own two eyes.

This didn't mean that I believed in psychic abilities, that people can communicate with the dead. The average person can see spirits and they don't have to be a medium to do so. When spirits want to be seen, they will find a way to manifest, no matter who you are.

I have always watched shows with psychics and mediums on television; ghost-related programs as well. Even though I was a skeptic, they still fascinated me. Everything paranormal got my attention due to my past experiences. Even though I had psychic and mediumistic experiences, I didn't realize they were my own abilities. I just thought they had come as a result of what was happening on the outside. When referring to psychics and mediums that I had seen doing readings on television, I would say, "That is a bunch of nonsense. They are getting the information before the show starts, and then they plant people in the audience."

Now when I think back on it, I realize how improbable that

was. There have been many readings on the air with countless numbers of people. Thus far, I have never heard of anyone coming forward claiming that they were paid to be a fake sitter in the audience. Not that there aren't plenty of phony psychics and mediums out there, but those people most likely keep a very low profile. I don't feel that they would expose themselves on television; they would be under too much scrutiny and watched very carefully.

My niece, Linda, bought a psychic reading for me for my 29th birthday. She paid $20 for it and also purchased one for herself. The readings were done in person. The house host set up reading events with a psychic and then would be paid a percentage of the money the psychic made for that day.

When we arrived at the house where the readings were to be held, we were told to walk in and be seated. The place didn't feel inviting. It was a bit dusty, lacked any attempt at decorating, and was very dull – not eye-catching at all. The atmosphere was stuffy; it felt like you couldn't breathe. There was a strong smell of tobacco added to the already thick air. I didn't count exactly, but there were about ten women sitting in the living room waiting for their turn to be read. The readings did not last long. They were each 20 minutes or less.

While we sat waiting our turn, the expressions on everyone's faces seemed to say the same thing. We all appeared to be thinking: *Why am I here? Is this woman for real? Are we just being taken in?*

I was the only male in the room. I thought, *I guess women are more into this stuff than men are.* My niece was called in first for her reading. It was a separate room; when she entered, they shut the door. I just sat there waiting for my turn and feeling a little uncomfortable, while the group of women gawked at me.

116

This was not Linda's first reading from this psychic. Linda told me before the reading, "Uncle Freddie, this woman is good. She has told me things that are true and that have come to pass."

I gazed at her with the look of a loving uncle. "Okay, dear. I believe you." But, deep down inside, my skepticism was solid; I went along anyway, for her sake.

When my niece came out of the reading room, her eyes were a bit red, as though she was about to cry, or had cried already. She sat down beside me and I asked, "What is wrong, Linda?"

She answered in a tone that was full of worry: "The psychic told me things about my job that I didn't like. She said that they will be letting people go and I was one of them."

Feeling protective of her, I answered, "Oh, forget it, Linda, don't let that upset you." I didn't want to expose her to what I really thought. Also, we were still in the company of those other women.

"She told me some other things I know to be true," she said. "But I don't want to believe them!" Linda has always been a believer in psychic abilities, and I feel she is a bit sensitive herself.

Now it was my turn to go face this ... psychic. I walked in and tried to sound friendlier than I felt. I said, "Hello, how are you?"

She said "Fine and you?"

"I'm doing okay," I replied.

She asked me to sit down; there was a small table between the two of us. Again, the room was very plain. It consisted of two chairs, a table, and curtains on the window. "Do you have any

117

questions?" she asked.

I answered, "No, I do not."

She suggested: "So how about a short general reading?"

I answered, "That is fine, thank you."

I noticed that she was using regular playing cards. I thought that she would be using Tarot cards, as I had seen on TV. She gave me an odd look. Being empathic myself, I felt she had picked up on my skepticism.

I cannot remember what the psychic said. What I do know is that the psychic could not read me. Everything she told me just didn't fit; basically, she gave up on me. She told me the reading was over and thanked me. She did not offer me a refund. I got up feeling very dissatisfied; the experience confirmed to me that what she claimed to be doing was a bunch of baloney. I thanked her and walked out of the room.

I rejoined Linda and she asked me, "How did it go?"

I didn't want to hurt her feelings about the sweet gift she had given me, so I told her, "It went well. Thank you for this birthday gift. No one has ever given me a gift like this before." I played it off, as if the information was private to me, and said, "I don't want to talk about it."

Today, I understand why some of my readings don't go as well as others. When a sitter is skeptical and closed up, it's very hard for the psychic to break through those barriers. The sitter has to be open to the reading, so that the energy can flow freely and the psychic is better able to pick up on the information that is coming to them.

An example of that comes to mind. I saw it happen once when I was watching an exceptionally gifted, world-renowned psychic medium who was a guest on the Oprah Winfrey show. She is someone I truly admire. There were two women in the audience who agreed to have a reading. One was obviously open to the reading, while the other one clearly was *not*.

The reading with the open-minded sitter was impressive and went very well. On the other hand, the reading with the skeptic did not go well at all. Everything the medium told her was challenged. "Oh, come on, a father always calls his little girl little princess," the sitter accused. The reading continued in this way, so that no matter what the medium said to her, it was questioned and rejected. It was clear that the medium was getting a bit frustrated; she explained, "I am trying to give you an experience here." It was useless; the woman wasn't going to budge.

This was an extremely gifted medium. I have witnessed her reading successfully on television many times, and I have a very high regard for her. I couldn't help resenting this sitter's closed mind and her intentional effort to discredit the medium publicly. It's one thing to be a skeptic, but when you don't even give someone a chance to validate their work, it is another. It got to the point where the medium said: "It's over, I am not going to waste my time anymore," and the reading was terminated.

I have thought about that gift from my niece, my first reading, all those years ago. Every time I see a psychic on television, or pass a psychic reading parlor on the street, I am reminded. I realize now that I was so closed-minded that I robbed myself of receiving the experience.

I did a search on psychic mediums on YouTube. Several videos came up. There were a lot of videos with titles beginning with, so-and-so "was debunked as being a fraud." I viewed a few of them. Some of the so-and-sos who came up were world-renowned psychic mediums. I felt it was unjust to call them a fraud just because they weren't correct at that particular time. Readings are affected by the openness of the sitter to receive, and by other outside circumstances; gifted psychics are human, too, and not immune to imperfection.

It is hard to fool a person who is experienced with readings. If the reader is a fake who uses *cold reading* methods, I would know immediately. A cold reading is when a fake psychic tries to fish for information during the reading. These fake psychics are very devious and cunning. They are the ones who have given true psychics and mediums a bad reputation.

I have nothing against skeptics. I feel that they keep the phonies in check. But if you are going to be a skeptic, be an open-minded one.

My life has changed in ways I couldn't have imagined. One thing is for sure: I am no longer a skeptic. I always tell the skeptics: "Okay, that is fine, but when we meet in the afterlife, I will tell you, see, I told you so." If they end up going to the afterlife before me, maybe they will come to me and say, "You were right!"

I joined a spiritual forum on the Internet so that I could practice and share experiences with like-minded people. About half of the participants were only there to receive readings. I noticed that many of the members (about 50 percent) who were giving readings were using different tools to help them gain insight. Some members were using pendulums, runes, angel cards, tarot, and other divinity tools. It was fascinating to me; I wanted to learn more about these different types of instruments. I read up on them and concluded that I wanted to use the tarot. I felt that the tarot would open my psychic abilities more, and I felt that I was guided to use this tool.

I went to the library and checked out several books on the tarot, and I spent my days studying them. The tarot has 78 cards; each card has an upright and reverse meaning to it. The meaning of the card changes whether it's right-side up or upside-down when you deal it out. A card that is right-side-up generally represents positive changes. A card dealt upside-down usually represents more challenging changes.

I decided to buy a deck, so I went to the Botanica. The only deck they carry is the *Rider Waite*, which is what I wanted — perfect — the Rider Waite is the most common deck used.

Many of the traditional card interpretations bear a striking similarity to philosophy found in the Kabala or in Alchemy. The literature regarding the tarot specifies elements that must be present in each card for the deck to be proper. There are custom or themed tarot decks that have an abundance of specific symbolism. These are more common in the predominantly English-speaking world, and are frequently created by amateur philologists. These are linguists who believe they have new insight into the proper analysis of the Kabala and Alchemy texts.

Each card has several meanings, and the reader determines which meaning they should apply based on the card's location in the spread and which cards are turned up around it. Common sense prompts the reader on which meanings to use or to discard, depending on relevance to the question asked. There are a variety of symbolic meanings that have evolved over the years. One example of how detailed a card can become is the *Major Arcana* card "The Moon."

This card has several elements, including a *crawfish* (or lobster) that is usually drawn very small, but is rarely omitted. Artists are free to represent these elements in any way they choose. They usually try to draw the picture in such a way as to reveal a new truth.

121

I thought, *How am I going to remember all of the meanings, all 156 of them?* I found out that some readers use only the upright meanings when reading. Later, I discovered that an experienced and knowledgeable tarot card reader will use the whole deck, upright and reverse. They would know how to interpret each card in relation to the other cards that turn up.

Since I couldn't remember each of the meanings of the cards, I bought a tarot card deck that had the meanings written on the cards themselves.

There are tarot card readers who have not yet reached their full psychic potential and/or are not mediums, so they use the actual meanings of the cards in their readings. I didn't want to read the tarot or give out information in this manner. I knew, because I was a psychic medium, that when I held the card I would feel certain things. It would trigger my psychic impressions to a higher degree. I used the *Celtic-Cross* spread. That is, I would turn a card over on the tarot card spread, but I wouldn't use the exact meaning for the card, whether it was right-side up (upright) or upside down (reverse).

I realized when I was giving my second tarot card reading, that my psychic impressions were greater than the information on the card spread alone. I brought through many more messages than I was expecting — a whole barrage of revelations.

Being very wet behind the ears with the tarot, in my readings I did incorporate the phrasing that indicated the cards' meanings in order to make the reading more genuine. It was, after all, a reading of the cards. But the reality was that it was my psychic impressions as well — what I was being told from the other side. I did, however, pick up only what pertained to the sitter. As I got used to the meanings of each card, I began to use my own wording in conjunction with what was printed on the cards. It took a little bit of time, but I did it.

122

Much of what I was giving during a first reading was validated at the time. Later, the sitter wrote to me and shared that a few things that had not yet happened at the time of the reading were currently happening. I was correct in saying that some of the things I told her had not yet come to pass. I thanked her for the confirmations she gave me. Again, I was amazed.

I wondered: *How did I get the names that I did in that tarot reading? And all of those other facts I told the sitter as well?* During tarot card readings, I felt a presence next to me. It was Louise, my mediumship-development spirit guide; she also serves as my gatekeeper. I was unknowingly receiving information about the sitter from Louise. At present, being more developed, I also receive symbols, images, and little movies in my mind's eye during a reading. Also, since I am clairaudient, I hear information – names, for instance.

When I gave names and descriptions of loved ones or friends, and they were validated, it made me feel ecstatic. I realized that I was listening closely and was truly receiving the messages. I learned that second-guessing or analyzing information isn't good for psychic mediums; we must trust the initial information we are receiving.

When I was still new at giving readings and very inexperienced, it was difficult for me to distinguish between physical beings and those who had crossed over; it was a bit confusing for me. As I advanced, I figured out that when I see a live person in my mind's eye, I don't feel an energy around me; I am picking them up clairvoyantly. When a spirit of a loved one comes through, I feel a bit faint. I feel their energy in a way that indicates that this person I am seeing and feeling has crossed over; nevertheless, they are actually there with me.

I kept doing tarot card readings on the forum and became

very popular — so much so that I couldn't keep up with the demand and it became a bit strenuous for me. I am not young anymore; I didn't know if this much energy drain happens to everyone when doing a reading or if age has something to do with it. I did find out through other mediums that it is normal to use a lot of energy while getting information from the other side. However, because of my empathic ability, the need to shield myself from absorbing too much emotional energy seems to drain me even more.

One day, I was listening to a radio station that is devoted to broadcasting everything paranormal. On that particular day, they had a world-renowned psychic medium on the show. He was giving out free readings to those who called in. I always liked listening to radio shows with psychic mediums because I was interested in hearing how they develop and grow; I feel the relationship I share with them. I decided to call in to find out if the medium would pick up on me and who I was and would give me some advice. This reading turned out to be a turning point in my life.

I actually got through on the call-in line and was thrilled. When they received me, I introduced myself as Freddie from New York City. The medium's reading for me was very accurate. What really shocked me was when he said to me, "Freddie, you have to put down the cards."

I could only say, "Excuse me?"

"Yes Freddie, you will be working with spirit, so this means that you can't use the tarot any longer." I was beyond surprised that he knew that I was doing my readings with the tarot! More than that, he was telling me that I had to let the cards go. I thought: *Put down the tarot?* It was like losing a limb, the tarot being torn away from me.

"Freddie, you did it before in the very beginning," he told me.

124

I did it before? What? I thought. Then I had an epiphany. The very first reading I did was when I helped in another online spiritual forum I frequented. The first reading I gave on the forum was to a woman who called herself *Country Girl*. She had lost her watch. I told her it was in a glass bowl, and that is exactly where she found it. I wasn't using the tarot then, or any divination tool; it all came from spirit. I was being shown what I could do, but instead, I had taken another path: the tarot.

The reading was uncanny in many ways. I thanked the medium for his more than insightful reading and hung up. I was terrified, to say the least, at the thought that I couldn't use the tarot anymore. For whatever reason, I had adopted the cards as a crutch. But in my heart I knew I had to follow what the psychic medium told me. I can't speak for other mediums, but I went through a period of self-doubt. I kept going anyway; nothing was going to stop me. I put the cards down and just used my God-given gifts.

Shortly after, I did a reading for a husband and wife. She was spooked by the reading. She asked me, "How do people react to the gifts you have; how do you do it and how does it feel?"

I told her, "It's very hard to explain. I give what comes to me at that moment, using all of my psychic abilities. I try not to second-guess myself. I get the messages from Louise, my gatekeeper, or directly from loved ones and friends on the other side."

She asked, "How does a spirit come to you and how does that feel?"

I answered: "I start to feel energy come in and my crown and third-eye chakra start to activate, and I know it's a spirit coming through. That's how it usually happens. I start to feel a little faint and then the spirit's image starts to materialize in my mind's eye."

She asked me this question because her husband's deceased mother came in during the reading. I immediately started to ask the spirit questions for confirmation and yes, the spirit was the husband's mother.

Incidentally, even though I had been told by the other psychic that I no longer needed the cards, I still did not feel confident enough at first. However, after this reading began, I started to pick up the third card and found that what the other medium had told me was indeed true. I was flowing along perfectly and realized I didn't need them. This was my last reading with tarot cards.

When I give a reading, I don't want to know anything about the person ahead of time. I only want their full name so I can meditate on them before their reading. I ask God to let me use the gifts that were bestowed on me to give the person closure and healing.

My understanding and ability to give readings continued to develop. Still, I knew that I had much to learn; there was a whole process ahead of me.

After the reading I had with the world-renowned medium, I became a bit troubled and anxious. *Spirit wants me to stop using the tarot* — I contemplated this repeatedly. Studying and educating myself, I knew that spirit guides don't make demands of you; they only advise you and allow you your freedom to choose. It is the law of free will and they do not infringe on it. They are very patient, to say the least. I knew that I would never stop being a psychic, regardless of whether I used tarot as a medium or not. I questioned how important this was to me: *Is this what I want to do; do I want to give readings?* I kept asking myself that question. I felt like a coward, a big chicken. The big word that was affecting me was *DOUBT;* this was the culprit — *DOUBT!*

Many autobiographical books I have read by highly acclaimed psychic mediums talk about doubt and how it affected them, especially in their early years. They speak about using reading-threads and forums by psychic mediums to foster their confidence and build their skills. You cannot be a successful psychic medium if you let doubt get the better of you. You have to kick it out the door. And believe it when I say: it takes some doing!

I debated with myself: *Can I really do this? Was this just a fluke? Maybe it's just here for a short time and then it will go away.* I continued this battle within myself. *But so many things have happened to me. I did do it, and my readings are very accurate. I do communicate with spirits.* The little angel and the little devil on my shoulders were at war.

I have always believed in God and Jesus Christ. My faith in God has grown in many ways, and it's not just in believing. It's a complete, definite, *without-any-doubt* believing! My experiences with Spirit and in life have now brought me to know, without a shadow of doubt, that God is alive and well. This fact, for me, is a direct result of my mediumship.

I could not explain away the information I received. There was no way I could know the facts – names, personal information about loved ones (whether crossed over or not), or about life events – that I receive during a reading. The things that come out of me are confirmed by the sitter. Events that have not yet occurred come to pass. I had to let go of all of that doubt.

Readings are just the tip of the iceberg; it's just one aspect of being a medium. Explaining to others what it is like for me is very hard, especially to skeptics who look at me like I am some kind of a nut. Am I imagining all of this? The answer to that is NO! For me, believing in myself and what I have experienced is the foundation of getting rid of doubt. I had to do the groundwork to bring myself to this understanding; but it did finally stick. God has given his children gifts that many can only read about in science fiction books, but to me and millions of others, it's a reality.

I have met psychic mediums who are in denial, or they don't want people to know about their gifts. It might be because of how we are sometimes treated by society. Some psychics rebuff who they are by saying, "I am not a medium but I communicate with spirit guides or other spirits, and I can see them." For many, it is because of their religion. Christians, for example, often interpret the Bible to say that communication with spirits is prohibited.

I wonder how much information a psychic receives from their spirit guides that they are not aware of. If they are telling themselves that they are not mediums and they are arbitrarily ignoring spirit communications, how much are they missing during their readings and throughout life? I cannot ignore a spirit or a loved one who is trying to communicate with me or the sitter. To me, I would be ignoring a gift that God has so graciously given me.

A medium can identify the source, while a psychic cannot.

Jack and Jeffrey

One day, I was on the Internet when I came across a listing on a search engine: "Make Money as a Psychic Advisor." I was curious and clicked on the link. I was directed to a website that offered many different kinds of advisory help, and one of those was for psychic and mediumship readings. I wasn't planning on becoming an advisor, but I wanted to see how it was done. There were hundreds of psychics and mediums listed with their expertise and biographies on hand and the ways in which they could offer their readings: via e-mail, chat, telephone or Voice Over Internet Protocol (VOIP). Their rates for readings varied and were listed along with the types of readings they offered.

I came across a listing of a gentleman on the service named "Jack." He was an English man living in Spain. Jack is a psychic medium, and his reviews are very good. Even though I was unsure of my interest in becoming an advisor, I was inquisitive about the service and how it was going for Jack. I saw that his availability button said "call me," meaning that he was open and taking calls for readings. I noticed that the call starts out free until the sitter feels that the advisor is the right person for them. At that point, if they choose to use the advisor, the sitter will click on a button that will start the reading and the psychic or medium will start to charge them.

The decision I made at that very moment was another life-altering change for me. It was one of those lessons that helped mold me into the person I am today. Spirit guides and angels assist us throughout life; but again, we have to ask for and be open to that help in order to receive it. Within the mysterious workings of God, our help often comes in forms we don't expect.

My Spirit guides knew that without using the tarot, I needed help concerning the readings. I decided to call Jack and ask him how the service was going for him. I wasn't interested in joining that service, because I wasn't ready to do that. I do feel, however, that I was guided to make that phone call to Jack.

I was feeling a bit nervous. I thought about what to say and how I should start off the conversation. I decided to just introduce myself and talk to him about his reviews and see where it went from there. I clicked on the "call me" button, and after the third ring he answered.

"Hello, this is Jack." his voice was refreshing. I don't often meet people from Great Britain in New York City, so I hesitated for just a moment when I heard his accent.

We spent a couple of minutes getting acquainted and then I said, "I am a bit embarrassed about this because I am not calling you for a reading, but to ask a question. I wanted to know how it's going for you, using this service to give readings. I am a psychic medium and I was thinking of joining the service sometime in the future."

He told me that he had only been on the service about six months and things had been very slow.

I couldn't believe how nice Jack was about all of this. I spoke to him sympathetically and asked him what he thought might be the problem.

Half laughing, he said, "Being that I am new to this service, I don't have many reviews yet. People tend to use the psychics that have a considerable amount of reviews. There are many talented psychics here and gaining a reputation by acquiring positive reviews takes some time. I have to be patient. My guides tell me that I am not very patient."

I didn't want to keep him because he could have had someone interested in using him while he was talking to me. Before I could let him go, he interrupted me to ask, "Why aren't you joining the service now?"

When I told him I didn't think I was ready, he asked why I felt that way.

"I haven't been a psychic medium for very long. Well I have always been a psychic medium, but I just recently came to understand my mediumship." I felt a bit embarrassed asking about a service when I wasn't ready for it yet.

Jack started to read me. What he told me was completely correct about everything. Jack doesn't use divination tools, he does the types of readings Spirit wants me to do: mediumship readings without tools.

I apologized for imposing on him; I had not called for a reading.

"Don't worry about it, Freddie; I feel that I am doing this for a reason. Spirit is telling me to do it. I need to tell you certain things and I am compelled to do so. Do you mind?"

"No, I don't mind at all, thank you."

Jack went on then: "I get that yes, you are a psychic medium and, as you said, you just recently rediscovered your mediumship. You came here because you were guided here for a reason;, you need help and you have doubt that you can do what was asked of you. Spirit has guided me into starting a website. I started it just two weeks ago and I already have over two hundred and fifty members. I have a great feeling that you will find what you are looking for there, and I would love for you to join."

Jack told me more about his website and I became excited just hearing him talk about it. His website wasn't like a forum; it was much more than that.

While we were still speaking, I went on the website and signed up. I saw that his site needed some help as far as graphics go. I told him that I am a graphics artist and I would like to contribute and donate to his site by designing some graphics. He was delighted and grateful. I felt that I had been guided to help him as well.

Jack and I ended the call and I started to go through the site. Everything was psychic and mediumship related. It was interesting and educational. Members wrote blogs, uploaded videos and music, and the site had a built-in forum.

Upon spending time in the forum, I started to make friends – lots of them. They are an online community of psychics and mediums, and I was in my element. Each member on the site has their very own page, profile, a photo of themselves, and a lot of other information. Being a graphic artist, I was able to design my own page easily and I received a lot of compliments. Most of the members are from outside the U.S.A. I was one of the very few American's on the site: Approximately 80 percent of the members are from England or from some other country in the UK. I became educated in "British English" and learned a variety of words not commonly used in the U.S. It was fun to learn the difference in what we call things, such as "flat" instead of "apartment."

I noticed that a lot of these psychics advertised on their pages that people could purchase readings. I wasn't about to charge money for readings. I knew I was in no way ready to do that. I knew I needed to study and learn *how* to give the information I received from the Other Side. I didn't know how to decipher or relay those messages yet. It's not like writing out a reading as I did when I used the tarot; I had to learn to take my time and articulate the reading in a professional way. It was important to me to do it the way Spirit wanted me to, and I was determined to do just that.

One day while I was on the site, a light bulb went on in my head. *Why don't I offer free readings on the site for those that want one? This is an excellent idea.* As I began to think further about that notion, I decided that I didn't want to do e-mail or "chat" readings; I wanted to hear a voice. Since most of my sitters would be from England and the rest of the UK, I decided to use Voice over Internet Protocol (VOIP). It was a very well-known service in the UK, as Skype is today. It was perfect. As long as the person had an account with the service, the call was totally free of charge. My only concern was, since I was in New York City, there was a five-hour time difference. I thought this could be a problem, but it worked very well.

I wrote up a narrative for my offer, saying, *"Hello all members, I am currently studying mediumship readings and I was wondering if you would help me out. I am offering free readings to those that would like one. I am in New York City and will use Voice over Internet Protocol (VOIP) to do the readings."* Since I wouldn't have to pay anything for the call, I could stay on as long as I needed to complete the reading. I continued with my post: *"You will need a headphone that will allow you to listen and respond. Please send me a message if you would like a reading and we can schedule a date and time, thank you."*

I waited a few days to see if I received any requests; then, on the third day, I got one. A gentleman by the name of Jeffery responded. He wrote: *"Hi Freddie, I am most willing to help you out. This is a good idea of yours. Have you received many requests from others? I do have an account with the VOIP service you use, and a headphone. When is a good day and time to have the reading done?"*

I was elated to get the request, but at the same time, I was terrified. I wrote back *"Hi Jeffrey, thank you very much for helping me out. I am free this coming Wednesday at 2 p.m. That will be 7 p.m. your time. Please get back to me if this works for you, if not, please let me know a date and time when you will be free."*

Jeffrey got back to me almost immediately. *"Freddie, the date and time you specified works for me. I'm sure you will do just fine with the reading. Talk to you then."*

At this point, I was even more petrified. *Okay, I have to do a reading; relax Freddie,* I told myself. But as the day got nearer, I became more anxious; I was very nervous. I guessed that was normal, since it was the first time I was doing a reading by voice and without using the tarot. I was trying to be pragmatic so I decided to have a self-talk: *Why am I nervous? The reading is free and he knows that I am studying — so stop it.*

I didn't want to be stuck by the computer giving readings with a plug-in headset. My computer was Bluetooth-enabled, so I bought a wireless headset that allows me to give the readings from anywhere. I decided on my living room sofa. I also wanted to record the readings so I could use them as a learning tool. I purchased a piece of software that would allow me to record VOIP conversations; I could record the reading for myself and also offer a copy to the sitter. I was "hooked up," everything worked great; I was ready.

The day came to give Jeffery his reading, and I was pacing back and forth in the living room. I talked to God and my spirit guides and asked them to help me relax. I wanted so badly to do what was expected of me: help people with the gifts I was given. Being a psychic medium was extremely hard for me in the beginning; I was plagued by self-doubt. It was easier for me when I used the tarot because I had a starting point. I had used the tarot as my launch-pad, a helping tool. Now, I had to receive information using my mediumship. I knew what I could do, it was already evident. I just made up my mind to go forward with it.

It's vital to have full trust in one's gifts and Spirit. A psychic medium must never second-guess what is coming through;

we must give the first information we receive. I did second-guess the information I was getting, though, in my very first readings. I've heard other experienced mediums talk about the same thing. It seems to be natural to do that in the beginning.

I was waiting near my computer when the VOIP software rang, right on time. I could see that it was Jeffrey. I had rehearsed how I was going to proceed, but I felt so nervous, it all left me. I took a deep, calming breath, whispered another quick prayer and began to calm down a bit: "Hello, Jeffrey?"

We exchanged greetings, and he agreed that I could record the session. I would provide him a copy. "This is my very first reading not using the tarot; I am a bit nervous as you can tell." I laughed.

Jeffrey chuckled. "You don't sound nervous at all."

"I am going to go into a slight meditation and call your energies to me." I told him.

I learned how to do this by studying. These days, I communicate with Louise before I start to read. I talk to her about the person I am going to read for beforehand; just their name and where they live. It's not necessary because spirit knows all, but I do it anyway. I ground myself, say a prayer, and place a white-light bubble of protection around myself. Then I ask Louise to come near me, right beside me, so I can establish a link.

Reading in person is the best way to read. Because the sitter is with you, accessing their energy is instant. The information comes through much more powerfully. There is no place for doubt and you must never second guess yourself. Most of all, you must have full trust in Spirit.

"Jeffrey, the first thing I am getting is that you are not married."

He responded that was correct.

"You have never been married?" Here I asked a question. Now I know I shouldn't ask questions during a reading. This is a cold-reading technique that is used by fake psychics. I had to learn to be definite in my readings; I go strictly by that rule now. Instead of asking Jeffrey, "You have never been married?" I should have said, "You have never been married".

There are times when a question is allowed. One example is when a name comes through but the reader can only hear the first letter of the name. The reader will tell the sitter: "I am getting a name, but I can only hear the first letter or the sound of a name that starts with the letter N; it sounds like 'Nor.' I feel that this person is close to you. Who is this person?" These are the kinds of questions I will ask. On this particular occasion, the sitter acknowledged that it was his cousin, Norma.

Jeffrey added, "I was married once."

I told him that I got that he was single at the present time. He confirmed that I was correct.

"Okay, I see you by yourself; I don't see anyone around you concerning a wife or a girlfriend, but I do get that there is someone you are interested in, but you are hesitant to make a move."

Jeffrey confirmed again that this was accurate.

"I feel that you are having health problems."

Jeffrey was puzzled "No not at the moment, as far as I know, I am quite fit."

"Okay, be sure to write it down, and please have a checkup."

"Thank you. I will do that."

I moved on. "I see a car, a champagne-colored car."

Jeffrey said he did not have a car in that color.

At this point, I started to have a heavy feeling of doubt. The information I was giving appeared to be wrong. I kept going, though. I told myself to stay calm and focused; I was practicing. Even knowing this, I unintentionally began to fish for information. It reminds me now, of the movie *Ghost*. The scene when Whoopi Goldberg's character was reading for a Hispanic woman and Whoopi started to say to her: "Did she know someone by the name of Anna?" and the woman says, "No, I don't know an Anna." Whoopi continues, "I am getting a Consuelo," and the woman says, "No, I don't know a Consuelo.' Whoopi keeps going: "Is it Julieta?" While Whoopi was saying the names, the sitter kept shaking her head no. "Is it Lucita?" and Whoopi rattled off a few more names until she came to the name "Maria?" The sitter replied, "Oh yes, Maria." This was a very funny scene, unless it is your reality, in which case it is not so funny.

"Or red," I went on, a far cry from champagne. "Purple, maybe." I didn't realize what I was doing.

Finally Jeffrey said, "No, it's blue." I felt like I wanted to hide my head under a rock or beat myself in the head with one.

Now I know that Jeffrey had an acquaintance that drove the champagne-colored car.

"I am seeing a rainbow, like a rainbow colored flag."

"Yes." he replied. "My website has a rainbow on it, the top banner." *Ah, finally something viable!* I thought.

"I get a name and it starts with a 'J', like a 'Joe' or 'Joseph.'"

Jeffrey accepted the name Joe.

"Yes, Joe came in first. Is Joe a good friend?"

He sighed. "Ah, it's going back a long way; it's more like a relative than a good friend."

"A relation; is he a cousin of yours?"

"Yes, he is."

I told him: "He is thinking of you and is planning on contacting you very soon. It might have something to do with money; I saw a money issue. Does that ring a bell with you?"

"Yes, it does; if he can give me some that would be nice." He laughed.

"I saw a house; you are planning on buying a house. There is an issue with this house."

He answered, "No, I am not buying a house, but I have just given one away; I had to give it to them."

"It's a very beautiful house, a very large house."

Jeffrey agreed. "Yes, yes."

"I don't get that you felt good about giving that house away; it really hurt you and it was a legal matter."

"It did hurt me and yes, it was a legal matter."

When I said, "There was a dispute," he acknowledged that was true.

"Do you have a cat?" I asked this question because what I was getting wasn't a physical, living cat; it was a bit confusing for me.

"No, I don't, but there is one in spirit."

"The cat comes around you. Have you ever felt the cat around you?" I asked, but he said he hadn't.

"I get that the cat has become a totem animal for you. Do you know what a totem animal is?" He did.

"You just received a telephone call. I saw a telephone and I am getting that some sort of deal will come through for you or has already come through."

"Yes, I did get a telephone call, but the issue is still unresolved,"

"I am getting an 'S' name like 'Silvia.'" When he hesitated, I said, "Silvia or Sandra." As I have said before, at times the sitter doesn't remember knowing a person by the name I give. Later they are able to confirm it. I have had many experiences like this.

Since he still didn't recognize the names, I suggested he write them down and he did.

"You are thinking of taking a trip."

"I am waiting for a call to see if I can go on a trip."

Once again, he confirmed the accuracy of the information when I said, "This trip will be in one of the countries in Europe."

"The name of Carmelita came to me. I feel this has to do with Spain."

Jeffrey exclaimed, "Yes, yes! I am waiting to hear."

"I saw Spain and heard the name Carmelita. Let me see if I get anything else on Spain. Yes, you are going to Spain, it's very positive. Hold on a second, I will see how your trip is going to turn out; it's going to be wonderful. It's going to be a very good trip, and you are going to enjoy yourself immensely."

"It's been a long time since I have enjoyed myself."

When I asked, "I am seeing a garage; do you have a garage?" he denied having one, but he added that he would explain afterward.

I asked if he knew someone named Norman. He acknowledged that he did.

"I get that Norman is in spirit."

"Probably; a lot of people I did know have crossed."

"Specifically Norman; Norman has crossed over." I felt a male energy around me.

Jeffrey responded uncertainly, "Possibly, yes."

"Norman is coming in. I feel he crossed over due to a heart attack. He has salt-and-pepper hair, but more on the light side."

"Yes, most of the people I knew are old and have provably passed on now."

"He is saying, "Hello, Hello.""

"Hello back." said Jeffrey.

"He says that he is sorry that he didn't spend enough time with you, Jeffrey. His job was demanding and he over-extended himself. This is the reason he developed a heart condition." I felt Norman's enormous energy and his image was clear in my mind's eye.

"Yes, I can understand that."

"He sends his love and he comes around you once in a while, but not very often. I get that you have sensed him."

Jeffrey affirmed, "Yes I have, as I have sensed a lot of people around me at the moment."

"Norman's energy is dissipating. A lot of people come around you and they get a lot of satisfaction from you. You help a lot of people connect with their loved ones and you help them to achieve closure. You have a good bedside manner, you don't ramble. People like that about you and they won't go to anyone else. Jeffrey, suddenly I see a park. Are you planning on going to a park?"

"Not that I am aware of at the moment."

"Because I see a park; it is some sort of gathering in a park."

141

"I can probably take that in another context," Jeffrey told me.

"What context is that?" I wanted to know.

"I can explain afterward, you are heading right on."

"Okay, great, so I will continue. You have a daughter; I see a female with light brown hair down to her shoulders, and parted in the middle. You have a daughter?"

"I have a daughter in spirit," he said.

"She crossed over, I am sorry. Did she cross over in her twenties?"

"No, she crossed over a long time ago; she was very young."

"Because she looks like she is in her twenties. Would she be in her twenties now?"

Jeffrey confirmed she would be. It was confusing to me because I thought I was picking up on his daughter who was still in her physical form. Her energy was very mild while coming through; most other spirits are more intense. I thought that I was sensing a person who was still physically alive. But I was really picking up on her *spirit*. Now I have learned that all spirits do not come in the same way. I have to ask the question from the sitter if this person is still with us if I don't feel that the spirit coming through has crossed over.

"She has a beautiful complexion; she is smiling at me. Did you name her before she crossed over?"

"Yes, we did."

Since I was practicing, I wanted to see if I could get more information. As a medium, I try to get as much information

142

as possible from the communicator (the spirit that is coming through). My goal is to prove that the consciousness survives after the death of the physical body. I am an *evidential medium*. An evidential mediumship reading usually begins with messages that give you evidence that your loved one in spirit is truly communicating with the psychic medium.

The reading with the psychic medium usually starts with substantial physical evidence. Examples of this are: what your loved one looked like, how he/she passed, age, names and sex of the person. Following that information, frequently the reading will include the description of their loved one's personality, likes and dislikes, and other unique characteristics about them that function as proof that it is truly that loved one who is coming through in the reading. They will also probably describe an account of how the loved one grew up, their family situation, marital status, and any children or pets that the loved one may have had. Often, the psychic medium will even use words or expressions that your loved one would characteristically use.

The intention of evidential mediumship is to support you in overcoming any skepticism you might have regarding the reading. Evidential messages leave the sitter with no doubt that it is their loved one who is coming through. They know that there is no way the medium could receive the particular information without having direct contact with them. After the evidence has been conveyed, the psychic medium continues with the rest of the communication. It may be something meaningful or not, but regardless, it offers the sitter further proof that this is indeed their loved one.

I went on, "I am going to try to get her name, hold on. I am getting a 'J' name like 'Joan' or 'Jonell.'"

Jeffrey said only, "No."

"I am not getting her name?"

"It was Lisa."

"Lisa?" Her energy was so mild that it was hard for me to understand her. I mentioned to a medium friend of mine from England about this experience. He told me that if I want to feel their energy in a more powerful way, I should ask the spirit to come closer to me. Just as in life, some people hesitate to get near a person they do not know; some loved ones react the same way in spirit and the medium has to gain their confidence. You need to say something that will give them a reason to get closer to you. Other spirits rush to the medium, afraid that the medium will go away before they have the chance to communicate with their loved one. These often overwhelm you. They want to get their message to the sitter quickly. They will try to jump ahead, in front of other spirits, in order to be heard.

"Jeffrey, I cannot get much from Lisa and she is now going away." It was important to me that I do a good job on my part. I wanted to give Jeffrey the absolute truth.

"I understand, Freddie."

"I see books, lots of them."

He acknowledged that he did have a lot of books and I added, "You are a very learned person, and I see you giving lots of readings. You are not a television person at all."

"Yes, I am educated, and I do give lots of readings. I don't normally watch television, but lately I have been, just to give myself a break from the books."

144

"This might seem obvious, but most of your books deal with metaphysics."

"Yes and no, but I will explain later."

I thanked him and stated, "You have students. I see you in front of students, people that you are teaching or mentoring."

Jeffrey affirmed, "Yes, that is correct."

"It has to do with spirituality, you're a coach." Confirmed in this, I said, "That is wonderful; your students really look up to you. They have the utmost respect for you and they listen and adhere to everything you say."

"Yes, they do."

On a new tack I said, "Melanie, I just heard the name 'Melanie.'"

"Yes, I can take a 'Melanie.'"

"I am getting that Melanie isn't with us anymore; she has crossed over."

"Yes, that is correct."

"I see a lady; she has short black hair, an older lady."

"Yes, that is correct," he said again.

"Was she once your wife?" I asked.

"No, she wasn't."

"Okay, I see now; she was a family member of yours."

145

"I think so, yes, going back a long time."

I told Jeffrey, "I asked her what caused her to cross over, and she said she had a massive stroke." At this point, I was trying to get as much confirmation as possible. Loved ones who have crossed over don't care about giving evidence; they just want to convey to their loved ones that they are fine, show flowers, and other symbolic messages. They are not concerned about giving detailed information. I had to ask Melanie to please give me some information to prove to Jeffrey that it was her and so she did.

Jeffrey recognized the cause of Melanie's death and I told him. "She just wanted to say hello and to let you know that she comes around you once in a while and that she is fine; her energy is leaving me, she is gone."

It's still very exciting for me that suddenly I feel an energy and a face starts to emerge in my mind's eye. In the beginning it was almost impossible for me to explain it; I thought it was something that only another medium could comprehend.

I knew Jeffrey would understand and he did.

I stopped for a moment and Jeffrey said, "There is a young lady that is around me."

I thought it was a spirit Jeffrey was talking about. "A lady that is around you… she is around you now?"

"Not around me, she lives quit a distance from me."

I laughed. "Oh, I am sorry; I thought you were talking about a spirit. This is a love interest."

Jeffrey said eagerly, "Yes, yes!"

146

I thought, *Wow, I must have been doing well, since he is asking me a question.* *"Okay, give me a second; I feel it's an 'S' name."*

"No."

At this point, I had to relax so the information could flow through me. "I am not getting her name."

Jeffrey replied, "That is okay."

"She just got over a relationship with someone else."

"Yes, about a year ago."

I said, "She is open for another relationship, but in the beginning, she was having a problem going into another one. She is getting better; she had a bad relationship and began to distrust men. I am getting that you are very interested in her."

"Yes, you are correct and I am."

"If you really want her, I am getting that you have to ease up on her; don't pressure her, let her get used to you. I do see her coming around. Okay, is that good enough for you?"

"That is wonderful."

I ended the practice reading and asked for his feedback.

He said it was very good, but he had a few questions about the style I used. "When you do your reading, are you relying on your clairvoyance and/or your spirit guides at the same time?"

"I use clairvoyance, clairsentience, and clairaudience in conjunction with my spirit guides," I answered.

Jeffrey explained, "I work a bit different; I allow my gatekeeper guide to let all of the spirits come in at once. I can separate them, and I feel quite comfortable with that. To me, proof that the consciousness survives after death is very important. The more confirmation I give the better. I try to give confirmation of their personality as well. I use three senses to link in."

I was very interested and told him: "You have my full attention; this is very important and helpful to me, confirmation is very important. What three senses are you talking about?"

"I use the heart chakra, and also very much my solar plexus chakra. So I am not just picking up on the spiritual aspect of it, and the third is that I am picking up on the psychic aspect of it as well. I am picking up from the spirit and I am also picking up from the sitter. Sometimes getting information from the sitter's essence is very important, so the spirit will answer without my needing to ask the sitter.

Jeffrey told me that he had been doing readings for over twenty years. I laughed. "You are the first actual reading that I have done. You have a lot of experience. What do you suggest that I do?" I was so new at reading, I asked this question eagerly. I know now that each psychic medium develops their own unequally individual way of reading.

Jeffrey explained: "If you have a group in a circle, and one person observes and actually takes you into a meditation, you can do a chakra meditation. If you do this, open your chakra's one at a time. When you open your heart chakra, do so front and back; you will take your consciousness into your heart chakra. You may find resistance when you first start, and you will have to be well grounded. When you're actually in your heart chakra, you will feel as if you are moving up and down like a hot air balloon."

"I understand. I have been working on my chakras about once a week and I am still opening, healing, and aligning them."

"That is very good. Now, getting back to your reading; about the park you saw, I actually live in a caravan, you might know it as a trailer."

"Oh yes, a trailer! So in the UK you call a trailer a caravan; so it's a trailer park?"

"Yes, so that is where you picked up on the park; I am always moving around. The telephone call, the important one you mentioned that I am waiting for, is from a woman friend of mine; we are to go to a location to start some workshops."

"I am getting Andalusia, Spain."

"It's in Spain, but I don't know if it's Andalusia yet; I didn't get the name. The metaphysics (I am actually a psychologist) is something I am very interested in. When I do my groups, it's not just the psychic or spiritual side of things, it's personal development as well. I like people to feel empowered when they leave. I put a lot into the groups — the psychic, spiritual, and psychological, so they are well rounded. Going back to the name 'Joan,' my mother's name is Josephine and everybody calls her Joan."

"That is amazing, thank you for confirming that." I was elated to know that I had not been far off at all.

"You mentioned a heart problem. My oldest brother had a heart problem and so did my mother. My oldest brother crossed into spirit from cancer and my mother is not very well at the moment, but I don't talk to her. Whether she's passed or not I don't know."

I was stunned. "You must talk to your mother!"

"Yes, I must, but I haven't been with her since I was four. She had tuberculosis, and I had to go live with my grandparents; my grandparents actually brought me up, so my mother and I never bonded."

"Oh, I see."

Jeffrey spoke of his romantic interest: "The young lady I am interested in is actually from Chili. We have a language problem because she only speaks Spanish."

"That is very interesting because I got a Spanish feeling when you mentioned her, but I didn't say it to you. I should have."

"Freddie, there is a huge difference doing a reading by telephone and in person. It's very different in person because you pick up a lot more, and you're about three thousand miles away from me."

"I fully understand what you mean. How do you feel I did with the reading?"

"Overall you did very well, actually, considering the distance and that you just started reading. Yes, you did quite well."

Excited and grateful for his kind words, I thanked him and told him, "I want to study more of the mediumistic part of the reading. I want to pick up more from the spirit or spirits that are coming through, and give more information."

Jeffrey commented, "Yes, but I feel there is bit of apprehension with you when spirit draws close."

"True, I feel that it was because I was nervous. You should have seen me before you called," I laughed, "but I seem to have become a bit more relaxed further into the reading."

"A lot of mediums block themselves because of their apprehension," he said. "They don't want to be wrong. One needs to be relaxed and natural and not blocked. At times I make a mistake; it's my mistake because I didn't establish a strong-enough link. I always remind myself that if you don't make a mistake, then you can't learn. You have to be humble enough to accept that you are going to make mistakes, and you need to be open and willing to let people know that. Then your mistakes won't seem so bleak, instead of trying to be correct all the time."

"Exactly, I hate to use this term, but it's not an exact science. I am good with that now and accept it."

"I don't say it's not an exact science. I just say I am just as vulnerable as anyone in making mistakes. I don't want people to place me on a pedestal. I tell them that I am no different than anybody else."

"They are treating you like a celebrity of some sort." I agreed.

"Yes, yes, and I am not a celebrity. I am the same as they are. There was one place I went to do a reading service where they applauded me on the way in. It affected me the whole evening, because they thought of me as somehow above or more important than themselves."

"They were treating you like a guru; they had expectations of you and it threw you off."

151

"Yes. Oh, and the house you brought up; I actually divorced last year after being separated for two years. I gave the house to my ex-wife because we have a nine-year-old son; he needed a roof over his head. She got the house and I got the caravan and the dog," he laughed.

"Jeffrey, you are going to be very successful."

"That is funny you say that. A woman I was dating went to see a medium and that medium also told her that I was going to be very successful."

"Yes," I replied. "I feel good things all around you. People love being around you and to have that is very special."

"Yeah, thank you very much, that was very nice."

"I want to thank you for taking the time to do this for me. It was very educational, and I learned a lot from your feedback. I will keep studying; I am so grateful for your help."

"You are welcome Freddie, and again, you did very well."

We said our goodbyes and hung up. This was wonderful for me because not only did I learn a lot, it opened me up in certain ways. It was a good start. When the spirits came in, it was a spectacular experience. I felt the differences in the way they came through. I learned that they don't all come in the same way; the energies are slightly different. As for my unique style, I find that I work best when I allow my gatekeeper to set the pace for spirits who wish to come through. I could not have them come in all at once, as Jeffrey does.

Chapter Six
My Healing Place

"For all healing, mental or material, is attuning each atom
of the body, each reflex of the brain forces, to the
awareness of the divine that lies within each atom,
each cell of the body." - *Edgar Cayce*

In the beginning, I didn't know that one of the many gifts
that each of us possesses is the ability to heal ourselves and
others — a realization that came to me from Spirit. The gift of
detecting an illness in others is called "medical intuition."
This is an ability we can all develop. It is usually strengthened
when one attains a higher psychic level.

I know that psychic abilities can come and go; a specific
ability can become dormant if it isn't used often enough. But
it can be reactivated through development or, as my
mediumistic gift did, it may come back on its own. One
medium told me, "If you don't use it, you lose it," but I don't
believe that. I do believe that it is more common for a
person's psychic gifts to be mostly dormant. Millions of us
are not always acutely aware that our psychic gifts exist, but
we are still aware of them in a mild, intuitive manner. Since
my psychic gifts have hardly been dormant, I am considered a
natural medium.

One day while I was lying down, I went into a slight trance. I
call this a light astral trance when my astral body just slightly
leaves my body. I began to experience this when my
mediumistic gift started to activate again. I shared this with
other mediums and to my surprise, many of them also
experience this phenomenon.

While in this light astral trance, I saw many little windows arranged sporadically, or like in a grid on a black background, as though they were on a black wall of space. The black mass with windows was moving about and when I tried to focus in on it, it would sway in the opposite direction. If I looked at it from the right, it would move to the left and vice versa. It makes me think of a touch screen on a computer. I could see that there were a variety of things going on inside of each window, only in high definition. Each window had its own assortment of colors. I didn't know what I was supposed to do. I just observed them and tried to see what was going on inside each of them. They seemed to all lead to a different portal with a different activity.

I experienced the same thing on another occasion, only this time I instinctively willed myself to go inside one of the windows. I was able to focus on it and when I did, I was inside in a flash. It was so unexpected, similar to experiencing vertigo and yet at the same time, I was in full control and totally aware of what I was doing. It seemed familiar, as if I had done it many times before.

Inside the window, which had now become a room, it was mostly dim, but the walls had some sort of green fluorescent light emanating from them. I started to see people walking around the room, and while I could decipher that they were both male and female figures, I couldn't make out their faces. They were dark and shadowy. On the far side of the room, there was a man lying on a table. He was covered up to his neck with a white blanket and he looked ill to me. There was a shimmering gold light all around him. The entities in the room were milling around, busily undertaking a purposeful task; they appeared to be doing something to him. To my disappointment, I became so fascinated that I came back from my astral trance. I tried to go back but I couldn't; an astral trance has to happen naturally for me and for a specific reason. Later, I was enlightened about the purpose of these glimpses that fascinated me so much.

I decided that if this happened again, I would try to stay calm. To my relief it did happen again, and this time I decided to communicate with the others. I said "hello," and to my delight, someone said "hello" back. Unfortunately (and I am sure you saw this coming), I got excited again and instantly snapped back.

I was a member of the James Van Praagh website, and I decided to write about and post this experience on the message board. There are a lot of psychic mediums on that website, and I wanted to see if anyone else had experiences concerning those windows. In the beginning, I got responses such as, "What an experience!" and "Have you gone into other windows?" I still waited and hoped to hear from anyone who had had similar experiences to mine. Finally, I was sitting in my living room one day when all of a sudden I got an urge to look at the message board; there was one response to my post. I thought: *It is probably the usual comment, with questions about the experience.* But to my delight when I opened the response, I saw that I had finally received what I was looking for.

It started out, "Hello, Freddie R" (this is what I called myself on the site) "I know where you are going when you are entering the rooms in the windows; I would like to chat with you in the chat area concerning your post." I was immediately excited and hoped to find this person in the chat room right away. I was hoping to hear some important piece of information that would help me understand this puzzling experience; I prayed it was not someone who just wanted to chat who was also looking to know more. Thankfully, that was not the case.

I entered the chat room and lo and behold, there was the person who had sent me the request to chat. I'm referring to this person as *The Healer* to protect his anonymity. It is a good fit, although there was no indication of his being a healer in the original name. Spirit works in mysterious ways. I quickly said "Hello," as I was worried I might miss my chance to make the connection. We did connect, and following is the conversation as it ensued:

I told him that I had seen his message about chatting concerning my post. After a few pleasantries, we got down to the subject on both of our minds. He said he had been hoping to find me as I had hoped to find him; we both felt that it was through the work of Spirit that we had connected.

I said, "I have a feeling where I was. I feel like I was in a place where spirits go when someone dies."

The Healer replied, "I could tell you with certainty. I know exactly where you were. I know because I was there before and I asked the *exact* same question."

"Since I might not go there again, I ask you to enlighten me, please."

"The problem was, when I asked, I got so many opinions, it didn't really help clarify anything at all; it just caused more confusion. You can go back there, it's *your* room." He said.

I asked him, "What did they tell you? Is there a thread on this site, about it?"

"I don't know that, sorry. There may be."

I remembered something he had said. "What do you mean, 'your room'?"

He didn't respond to that but asked me, "Why would you not return?"

"I don't know; I am very new at this."

"No, you aren't."

Confused, I asked: "Do you think I will return to the room?"

He wrote: "I really do understand why you think you are new at this, but trust me, you aren't. I know with absolute certainty that you are fully able to go back there at will. How'd you get there this time?"

"I have a problem staying where I go; I get overwhelmed and excited and come back."

"I understand," he responded. "In the room there was a very long table, right, and very high ceilings?"

"The table I saw the person lying on? The table was long and yes, the ceilings were kind of high."

"The 'person' could be on the table," he agreed, "but the table is one like you might expect to see at the UN or somewhere – one that would seat a great many 'persons.'"

"No, I didn't see that. It was a room with people walking around. Farther back, I saw a younger person lying on a table who was covered, except for his head, with a white sheet. He had a gold illumination around him."

157

He described it as the "glow of light energy"; I assumed he was correct because I really didn't know what the "gold light" meant.

The Healer queried me further: "As though a soul is being healed? You recognized this 'person' as being dead, so what would the purpose be to 'operate' on that body?"

I ventured "He probably had a traumatic death."

"Does it sound true that he was receiving light energy to heal?"

"Yes, it does."

The Healer gave me a nudge: "Why do you think you might just 'stumble' upon this scene?"

"I have no idea."

"Does it sound truer that you have likely been there many times, but this particular time you remembered?"

"I have seen astral windows, but never entered."

"You have never entered that you remember," the Healer corrected me.

"This time I just appeared in the room. Yes, I guess that I remember. It was like I willed myself to go in."

"Think about the possibility that you only remember peering into windows before, but this time your recollection was being *in* the room."

"Yes, I popped into the room, surprisingly."

"Other times you withdrew to your physical reality."

I protested: "No, not willingly. It just happened because I became excited."

"We do much in that realm – we go more times than we recall."

"I understand. What was that room?"

The Healer explained: "A healing room, exactly what you perceived it to be. A healing room, just as you said. Why do you think you would be there?"

"To heal?"

"You weren't the one being healed, exactly. You are well on your way, friend."

"To what?" I enquired.

"No one can explain it to you better than you can to yourself. I can suggest something that may help you find answers. I will be truthful and admit that I have discovered on my journey that every answer brings with it more questions than I had to begin with, but you will get the answers you need. So, keep practicing astral, but try this, when you set out to 'go,' have the intent to seek the counsel of spirit guides and helpers."

Nervously I asked: "So, there is something wrong with me?"

"Not at all, to the contrary, there is something *right* with you."

159

"So, I have a purpose. Do you think that I am a healer? I keep getting that in my mind."

"You would not have been present otherwise, would you? You were not there to be healed, right?"

Tentatively I confirmed, "I am a healer."

"Yes, you are! You know your truth. Knowing and accepting are totally different than understanding, aren't they?"

I told him, "Let me tell you a story: My mother fell in the kitchen and hurt her leg. Yesterday, her knee hurt very badly. She asked me to pray for her. I grabbed her hand and placed my hand on her head and prayed and now, her pain is gone."

When the Healer asked if I was surprised, I answered, "Yes, I am, because I didn't know what being in that room meant. I suppose no one goes in there unless they are healers themselves."

"Hmm, well, let me ask you this: Where did you get the idea to touch her in the way you did? What prompted you to know what to do?"

"It just came to me, like instinct."

"Exactly, and you chose to follow through."

"But I didn't know that I have gone to that room many times, seeing someone on that table. I didn't realize it."

"There is nothing 'wrong' with you. You've been in that room many times. You just did not bring that consciousness back with you every time; it's like remembering dreams. You

160

won't remember *everyone*, but when you are ready for the lessons, you will recall."

I wanted to know what lessons.

"You are learning who you are. We are all part of a team that is much bigger than we could imagine."

"What do you do? You are a healer too; I sense it." His true name on the message board did not indicate that he was a healer.

"I am at home now. I am an online merchant as a job. Yes, I am a healer. I am a Light-worker, the same as you. There are many of us. It's just that many don't remember in the physical realm. We are beings of light in spirit, sharing a human existence."

(A Light-worker is a person driven and motivated to do work with Spirit to make the world a better place. They improve their own and other people's lives through elevating their consciousness to higher levels.)

"You have to forgive my ignorance, I am new to this. Knowing, that is." I confessed. "Can we heal ourselves?"

"The concept of 'ourselves' is very misleading in my opinion."

"Enlighten me, please?"

"You are not as limited a creature as you might think. This is why I think it would be good for you to seek the counsel of your team. You might be very surprised at how many different entities comprise *your* existence."

161

"Being in that room was, I have to say, weird. It was so clear when I entered it and yet, I couldn't see the other people's faces. Why was it so dark?"

The Healer responded, "You'll come to know these answers. If I tell you what will happen, when you *do* ask your spirit guides the questions and they answer you, you will then wonder if it was a 'real' answer or if you are just being persuaded by my words. I could tell you the answer to everything that you ask. But if I tell you, it will leave room for you to doubt the answers. It leaves you to question whether you are experiencing something real or imagined. Sometimes it's best to get the answers directly from the source.

"I don't understand." I really wanted him to give me more answers. I fully understood the Healer now – he didn't want to influence me. "I know where I was. I was not imagining it; I never doubted it." I said.

"I have walked the same path, so I am only trying to help you find your way, the same way I was helped to find mine. You already know your answers, you just need them confirmed. You could ask a million people these questions and literally get a million different answers, and every one of those answers would be correct. Don't forget to keep practicing your journeys, they're important and it gets easier, you just have to practice."

"It's hard sometimes, staying where I want to stay for answers. I keep coming back too soon. Just as I start to ask questions, I come back."

The Healer was encouraging. "It will get better, think of it like math in school."

"I have to be patient."

"Before you could be taught long division, you had to be taught multiplication. Before you could learn multiplication, you had to learn addition and subtraction, right? As you begin to accept and understand, you will be given more awareness. If you get overwhelmed, you might have to shut down in order to protect yourself. Then you have a blockage to deal with."

"How do you deal with a blockage?"

"Trust that it will get better with practice. You keep practicing; each tiny bit you learn removes the blockage. You wouldn't want to turn on the water spigot of your kitchen sink and have the amount of water flowing through the city pipes come out at once. You'd be flooded."

"I seem to be getting better at getting there, but staying there is the problem." I complained.

"You are there longer than you remember. You are always there, and you're just becoming aware of it at this level, just like the water is always flowing at the same rate it is in the city pipes."

At this point I felt like a young monk learning from a master. "I just didn't remember being there, until now."

"Accept your truth," he said, "and more will follow it. Have faith; you are well, be blessed."

I thanked him and we said our farewells, agreeing that we might meet again in the future on the message board.

The conversation was a bit cryptic; it felt to me as if I was communicating with a spirit entity. I have asked a couple of questions to the Healer on the message board since, but I never got an answer again.

Who was this — was it a physical being or a heavenly one? I asked myself. I was tempted to ask the Healer if he was one of my spirit guides. I felt a bit silly, so I didn't. Maybe I should have asked the question; it certainly couldn't have hurt.

Now I know that there are people so enlightened that they communicate in this manner at will. Friends tell that I have changed the way that I speak. It is very different, they say, than the way I spoke before. When a person's eyes are opened, that person sees life and the universe in a very different light. I look at people in the streets and I think, *If they only knew of the gifts that God has given them.*

I went to that place with the windows (My Healing Place) about twice a week for approximately three months. For some reason, I have not been back there for about three years. I hope to return again.

Sometimes I meditate sitting on a chair. I have noticed, however, that when I lie down I am more relaxed and that seems to affect me; more transpires while I'm lying down. I see symbols, scenes, and colors. On one such occasion, about ten minutes into the meditation, I started to see a white silhouette of a human being on a dark background. It was a simple mental meditation, one that was without music or guidance, but it was performed in stillness. Suddenly a rainbow of colors appeared around it; it was an aura. It stayed there for only a couple of seconds and then it disappeared. After the meditation, I started wondering why I had the vision; I know Spirit showed me this for a reason. Spirit

164

always sends me a symbol to convey something to me. I was confident that I would find out soon enough.

The Aura Reveals

I was doing a reading and it was going well. The woman I was reading for was very open and her energies were strong; she was like an open book. At one point during the reading, I felt compelled to close my eyes. When I closed my eyes, I began to see the outline of a woman's body. Then the colorful aura followed as it did in my meditation. (Spirit was conveying this to me during my meditation when I saw the silhouette with the aura around it). I realized that I was seeing the body of the woman I was reading for in my mind's eye. Not only that, I began to see what looked like a dark spot around the kidney area. I thought: *Okay, let me see if this is what I think it is.* I had read and watched psychics on television being able to detect illnesses in people using several different methods. I decided to ask: "Do you have a problem with your kidneys?" The woman answered: "Oh my God yes, I do; I need a kidney transplant."

I can't begin to tell you how I felt; the feeling is indescribable. *This is incredible; this is what Spirit was telling me. I can see illnesses in my mind's eye.* This is what my journey through the windows is about. This is the message from Spirit. As more of my gifts are emerging, I am learning about healings not only for others, but also for myself. I can't see auras or detect illnesses just by looking at someone, as some psychics do. It is shown to me in my mind's eye instead. Who knows how this may evolve in the future.

Being a medical intuitive is very special to me. I do not advise or replace a doctor, but I can make suggestions to have certain symptoms checked out or particular areas of the body examined. Usually when I give a reading, at the end I offer a free medical scan. Because I am not a doctor, I have to be very careful about how I give this information. The person that I am reading for may not know of an illness they have, or of an illness that is beginning to manifest. For instance, if I get that one of my sitters has breast cancer, and I know it without any doubt, I can't just say, "I'm sensing you have breast cancer." Like therapists, psychics must be very mindful of the fragility of their sitters; news such as this would be obviously shocking and could be devastating. I will carefully say to the sitter, "I am getting that you have to see a doctor, and please have them check your chest area. I suggest having a mammogram. We psychics are human and we make mistakes, but please go have that mammogram." This was actually something I did have to tell a sitter. She called me back later and told me, "Freddie I had the mammogram, and they did find a small lump on my right breast. They did a biopsy and it was benign." I was very happy for her.

When I run my hand over an area of a person's body, I am able to detect troubled areas where illness could develop or has developed. Usually chakra areas on a person's body are cold when the chakra is unhealthy and needs to be opened, cleared, and aligned. If a person doesn't care for their chakra system, it can lead to illnesses, especially depression. I used to be depressed a lot, but when I started working on my chakras, the depression went away.

I am also a *Reiki Master*. Reiki (commonly called "palm healing" or "hands-on-healing") is an alternative healing therapy in which the practitioner channels and directs life-force energy through the palms of their hands to the meridian centers in the body. This technique transfers universal energy, which allows for self-healing and a state of equilibrium. In the next chapter, I will talk about how I have used the energy healing method known as Reiki. I will share how one such healing turned out to be a supernatural experience for both my client and me.

Chapter Seven
The Supernatural Healing of
Patricia Seward-Lazaro

"You may be an undigested bit of beef, a blot of mustard, a
crumb of cheese, a fragment of underdone potato. There's more
of gravy than of grave about you, whatever you are!"
— *Charles Dickens, A Christmas Carol*

Being a medical intuitive, I wanted to learn a form of energy
healing. I researched online and I found that there are many
different forms of this type of healing; the most common one
is Reiki. Reiki is a spiritual practice developed in 1922 by Dr.
Mikao Usui. After three weeks of fasting and meditating on
Mount Kurama in Japan, Dr. Usui established the ability of
"healing without energy depletion." A portion of the practice
(tenohira or palm healing) is used as a form of
complementary and alternative medicine (CAM). Tenohira is
a technique that practitioners use to move "healing energy" (a
form of *Ki*) through the palms.

I decided to start out with a course in Reiki and, to make a
long story short, I dove in all the way and I became a Reiki
Master.

My distant healings are done free of charge. Distant healing is
sending Reiki energy for the purpose of healing someone that
is not physically present. This technique is the Hon Ze Sho
Nen (Distant Symbol) in conjunction with other Reiki
symbols and a variety of other techniques: photo technique;
Reiki stacks; healing lists; or teddy bear technique – for a

169

point of focus. I use the photo technique.

The reason I use the photo technique is because I feel closer to the individual, even though I can't be with them in person. My distant healings are done for people living all over the world. No matter where they are, the healing energy will reach them at that precise moment. I advertise my healing (free of charge) on several psychic-oriented web sites. I ask those who want a healing to send me a photo of themselves with a self-addressed and stamped envelope. That way I can send them back their photo once I perform the healing on them. They can also e-mail me a photo, and I can print it out and use it.

One day in April of 2008, I decided to go on the James Van Praagh message board on his public website. I read some of the posts written by other members. I came upon one with the title "Someone Grabbed My Arm" by PattyL. On the post, she wrote: "I was sitting down in my living room and suddenly something or someone grabbed my arm. I really felt it; it was very real."

At the time, I was still using the Tarot to give readings. I decided to respond to Patty's post. "PattyL, I feel it was your husband, and I am getting a 'J' name like 'Joseph' or 'Joe.' I feel that he crossed over due to congestive heart failure."

PattyL responded to my reply and said, "Yes Freddie, my husband's name is Joseph, but I call him Joe. And yes, he died due to congestive heart failure in 2005."

When I replied back and gave her more confirmation about Joe, one of the things I told her that caught her attention was that she was a beautiful woman and that Joe loves her very much.

She answered: "Freddie, the other day I was sitting down

170

talking to Joe and I asked him, Joe, why is it that you never told me that I was beautiful? Now you come back and tell me that I am beautiful. This wasn't coming from you Freddie. Joe was responding back to me through you. Why did you say this, Freddie?"

I told her, "I don't know. It just came to me; I just felt I had to say it to you."

Patty and I kept corresponding with one another and we became very good friends. She and her husband Joe had moved upstate from New York City when they were married. They had no children together, but they both had children from previous marriages.

Patty always seemed very sad to me; I felt her sadness. Eventually she told me that she suffers from several illnesses and that she misses Joe so much that she doesn't want to keep living anymore. She wanted to "go with Joe already." I felt her pain. After that, I started to tell her about everything I do as a psychic medium.

I communicated with her almost every day. She was so interested in what it was that I did, that I felt that she was a natural intuitive; she had precognitive dreams. She always told me her dreams, and on many occasions they came to pass. I felt that she was gifted, but she didn't put a label on it because she never thought of herself as psychic.

After I became a Reiki Master, I wasn't sure when to start offering healings to the public. I knew that Patty had several illnesses, and one day I asked her if she wanted me to do a distant healing for her; I felt that Spirit wanted me to do it for a reason. Patty was overjoyed that I offered this, and she immediately mailed me a photo of herself.

On September 2nd of 2008, I spoke to Patty and asked her to

171

do several things before I started the healing. I asked her what time she usually goes to bed and she said at 10:00 p.m. I told her to please be as relaxed as possible while on the bed. She was a bit nervous about the healing and asked me if it would harm her in any way. I gave her a website where she could read up on Reiki to alleviate her concerns.

A Reiki session can encourage one to let go of tension, fear, anxiety, or any other negative feeling. It promotes peace and a state of wellbeing. It balances and harmonizes the entire system. When the body is in balance, it can heal itself. Reiki treats the whole person – body, mind, emotions, and spirit. It can be complementary to medical or psychological treatment. It can help to reduce negative side effects from chemotherapy, surgery, or invasive procedures. It can shorten healing time, reduce or eliminate pain, reduce stress, and it helps to create a more positive attitude. Most people experience deep relaxation, which encourages healing on all levels. Being in a relaxed state allows the positive healing energy to bring about a healthy balance. Reiki can help emotional trauma or anyone going through a stressful situation.

Reiki can also help those who are in good health to stay that way. It helps to keep stress at a minimum, enhances the immune system, and just helps the person to stay in a state of happiness.

This method of healing can never be used to cause harm because Reiki energy is guided by Divine Consciousness. Because Reiki is spiritually guided, the energy goes where it is needed most. It can be used as a complementary technique for any medical treatment. One cannot heal if one is in a constant state of tension and stress. Through Reiki, the vibration is raised and illness cannot live in that environment. It may take several sessions before health is restored to the physical body. Healing takes place on distinctive energy bodies, and it takes a while for all of the good healing and positive energy to filter down into the areas where it is most needed.

Reiki is being used in hospitals, and in elder and hospice care, and in all related medical fields. Insurance companies are starting to take a closer look at this incredible alternative therapy system because it is cutting down on patient recovery time. It reduces pain and anxiety for the patient as well as the need for pain medications.

I reassured Patty that Reiki could not harm her in any way. She became more relaxed and eager to get started with the Reiki treatment.

What I am about to tell you came to me unexpectedly. I had heard and read that while a Reiki practitioner is administering a treatment, they might experience paranormal events during the process. One medium friend of mine told me that while he gives a Reiki treatment, his Alchemy spirit guide stands by him and assists him. He actually sees his guide there with him throughout the whole process.

In order for a Reiki healing to be effective, the recipient will have to give consent for the healing. If this is done without a person's specific approval, the practitioner will be infringing on the persons free will, and the treatment most likely won't produce the desired result.

It's very important that we do not suggest starting or stopping of medications or to undergo a medical procedure; we are not licensed doctors. We can, however, recommend seeing a doctor and have the doctor concentrate on a specific area or areas. It's up to the person whether or not they want to follow our advice. There are licensed doctors who also practice Reiki or some other form of energy healing.

The day came to give Patty the healing. I waited until 10:30 p.m. to start since Patty was going to bed at ten that evening. I wanted to give her time to relax before I started. I lit a white candle and frankincense; then I sat down on my couch with her photo. Using a folded quilt on the left arm of the couch as an elbow rest, I made myself comfortable, sitting up straight with both of my feet flat on the floor. I started out with a prayer to state my intent to God: "Dear God, I sit here tonight as a healing vessel to send your beautiful healing golden light to one of your children, Patricia Lazaro of upstate New York. This is a photo of Patricia; she suffers from several ailments and has given me the permission to do this healing for her. I know, God, that you have given your children the gift of healing. Now let me use that healing gift as you would want me to. Thank you, God, for this healing gift. Amen."

I held Patricia's photo in my left hand and began to recite the Reiki healing symbol mantras. I repeated them three times each. The first symbol is the Usui master symbol "Dai Koo Myo"; the second symbol Usui Mental/Emotional "Sei He Ki"; the third, Usui Long Distance symbol "Hon Sha Ze Sho Nen," and the last symbol, which makes all the symbols much more powerful, is the Usui Power symbol "Cho Ku Rei." While saying this mantra, I outlined the Power symbol with my finger on top of Patricia's photo.

I then held her photo in between my two palms, rested my left elbow on the quilt, and started to relax. I meditated and waited to feel the healing energy come down into my crown chakra. When I started to feel a tingling sensation on my crown chakra, I knew that the healing energy was entering me; it was filling and enveloping my entire body. I channeled the energy gently to my palms, where I held Patricia's photo. It's a feeling that is indescribable. The only way I can put it is that it is a feeling of love, peace, and joy.

I started to see Patricia in my mind's eye. She was lying down peacefully. I was seeing the golden healing energy coming down to her from the sky. It was entering and becoming omnipresent in her body. I kept saying in my mind, "God, send your golden healing light to Patricia; I am your vessel. Thank you God, for your trust in me."

Twenty minutes into the healing, what occurred was remarkable. It continues to baffle me now. I wasn't frightened at all, and I didn't stop the healing despite it. Perhaps I was being helped by my spirit guides. They were making me feel that all was well; I need not be fearful. I just needed to continue the healing. I had felt three sharp tugs on the quilt under my left elbow. I paused in my talking to God and in sending the healing energy to Patricia. I didn't open my eyes, though. It couldn't have been my mother because she was in her room, and I would have heard her come into the living room. She wouldn't tug on the quilt that way anyway. I instantly realized that it was a spirit. Whoever it was, I wasn't ready to acknowledge them; I still had my eyes closed.

When I tell this story, some people laugh because I said in a whisper to the spirit, "Hold on, I will be right with you. I am not finished with this healing yet." At the time, I didn't find it funny. I still had my work to do and did not want to be disturbed. I ignored it and I kept performing Patty's healing. Suddenly a woman started to appear in my mind's eye. She looked like she was in her early seventies and had a motherly feeling to her. She was saying to me, "Thank you, thank you," with a warm smile. Telepathically I told her, "You're welcome." I didn't know who the woman was, but she resembled Patricia. I decided she must be one of Patty's family members, but she wasn't the spirit that tugged on my quilt. Whoever the woman was, she began to fade from my mind's eye until she was gone.

I started to feel the healing energy become less pronounced. That was a signal to me that the healing was coming to an end. I sat there for a few minutes before I opened my eyes, and then I sealed the healing by holding up Patty's photo and saying and outlining the Usui Power symbol with my finger over her photo three times; I was done.

I looked to my left towards a window in my living room that was five feet from where I was sitting. Next to the window there is a love seat, and sitting on the right arm rest I saw a man. He was transparent, but I could see his body and his face. The man kept focusing on my fan that was running next to the window; then he would look back to me. Again, I didn't feel threatened or scared in any way. If I had seen this before I regained my mediumistic gifts, I would have shrieked and run away. I have, of course, seen and communicated with spirits many times – but in my mind's eye. I rarely see a spirit with my two eyes, especially a full-bodied one.

I looked at his face and recognized who he was. Although younger, he was definitely Joseph, Patty's husband. I had been shown a photo of him. I said to him, "Hello, Joseph, how are you?" He didn't answer. If he had said anything, I would have heard him telepathically, but he didn't speak. He kept eyeing my fan. I remembered Patty telling me that Joe turns off appliances in her home and on some occasions turns them on.

Again, when I tell this story to others, they laugh. I told him "Joe, please do not turn off my fan, it's hot in here." He looked at me and grinned. He still remained silent and I thought, "I wonder why he's here?" At that point, he got up and walked across the living room right past me and slowly disappeared. I just sat there dumbfounded; this was incredible! What amazed me was the tugging on the quilt; it must have taken a lot of energy on his part to do that. After the healing, I felt a bit more drained than usual. I came to the conclusion that he must have taken some of my energy in order to tug on that quilt the way that he did. I began to cleanse myself with white light and thanked God for allowing me to do this healing.

The next day, I was curious to find out from Patty if anything happened while she was lying down during the healing. I saw that she was on the Internet, so I started a chat session with her. I was very interested in what happened to her while the healing was going on because of what I experienced myself; something had to have happened on her end.

When I asked her about her experience of the healing, she said: "I was lying down and at about 10:45, I began to see little lights above me, twirling. I just lay there. I wasn't scared or anything, then I just fell asleep."

I didn't know how to begin to tell her what I had experienced during the healing, so I just took it one step at a time. She was astonished, as anyone would be. She laughed when I told her about the fan. Then I began to ask her questions.

"Patty, when I saw Joe, he looked a bit younger, but I knew it was him. He didn't say anything."

"Yes Freddie, Joe was a very quiet person; he didn't talk much."

"That is probably why. I wonder, why did he come to me?"

"Maybe he was protecting me; I was a bit nervous about the healing."

"I don't think that was it; he was there, perhaps, to help me."

I have read others' reports of healings where they experienced seeing spirits. Some can be spirit guides and

177

some can be loved ones who have crossed over and are there for the healing.

I asked her about the woman I saw in my mind's eye. "Patty, the woman I saw had a round face; you look a bit like her."

"I feel that she was my grandmother. I have been told that I look like her."

"Yes, there was a motherly kind of feeling about her. She didn't stay very long; I guess she felt she didn't want to disturb me and left after only about ten seconds."

Six months later, I gave Patty another reading, and her grandmother, Esther, again made an appearance. This time, I was able to give Patty more information. Before Esther left, she threw a bouquet of roses at me for Patty, but while the roses were flying to me, they turned into daisies. I told this to Patty, and she told me that daisies are her favorite flowers.

When I do a healing, I have to do it without any doubt. My faith is strong and needs to be so. I feel that having complete confidence and strong faith are the foundations of healing. A healer's intent is also very important. I do healings because I want to help people. At times, a person is so far gone that a healing can only alleviate some pain. If it's your time to go home to God, there is nothing that can stop you from doing so.

Patty told me two weeks later that her health had improved immensely and that two of her illnesses had completely disappeared. One is still present, but it's fully under control, whereas previously it was not. When she told me this, I got teary-eyed and felt a lump in my throat.

Patty told me, "Freddie, your healing worked. I can't tell you how thankful I am to have met you. Before, I didn't want to live anymore. You have changed that; I want to live. Freddie, you have made my life so much more interesting, and I don't feel alone anymore, thank you."

I didn't know what to say. I simply told her that I was merely a vessel to do God's work. The healing I did on Patty strengthened my confidence in my path. I understood that in heaven, they know what I am doing and that my prayers are being answered.

Chapter Eight
Out of Control

"People are afraid to die, and even more afraid to live."
— *Sylvia Browne*

I have given a lot of consideration to how much I should write about the negative aspects concerning the spirit world. I mentioned earlier in the book that there is a duality between positive and negative to everything. This subject is rarely touched on by many mediums. I decided that this is something I should go ahead and share with you. Although most spirits are good or harmless, our lifestyles influence whom we draw to ourselves. I shared my story of the destructive entity who attached itself to me when I didn't take care of myself. When we overindulge in alcohol, do drugs, live a negative life style, and make poor choices, we make ourselves susceptible. Even being ill makes us more vulnerable to these lower vibrational spirits and we become their targets. Most of these negative entities are evil and want to do us harm.

Many times it is not the fault of the person who is being plagued by evil forces. Sometimes it is a matter of moving into a space that already harbors these entities. The movie *The Conjuring* is based on a true story of such a situation. It is about a family in 1971, who were experiencing increasingly disturbing events in their farmhouse in Harrisville, Rhode Island. A married couple, the Warrens, who are well-documented demonologist and paranormal investigators, came to assist the Perron family, who were experiencing frightening occurrences at their home. This was just one of the many cases they worked on.

My intention isn't to scare you, but to give you a message. Take care of yourself. The healthier we are, the stronger our aura will become. The aura is like a force field to protect us. If the aura is weak, it will make our vibration lower, and we will become targets. Lower vibrational entities use this to attach themselves to us. Being a happy and positive person will also reinforce the strength of the aura and heighten our vibration. I pray all the time, and that brings me closer to God, hence bringing highly vibrational White Light beings around me, including those in human form.

After Andreas appeared to me and the blockages of my mediumistic abilities were torn down, I once again began to experience what I had experienced as a child. I had a refreshing and enlightening new look at things. This time, I could identify what these things were, and I had begun to explore every experience I came across. I had a deeper understanding.

There was a woman in my building who lived on the floor above me. At first, while she was still a teenager, I saw her occasionally in the hallway with her mother. She was friendly and we smiled at each other. I had always felt drawn to her for some reason. I think she felt a connection to me because one day I had witnessed her mother being abusive to her in the hallway. Her mother was shouting obscenities at her and treating her very badly. I was affected by the inappropriateness of the way she was accosting her own child. I yelled at her mother: "Why are you treating her like that? I have a good mind to report you." The mother barely acknowledged me and without giving me an answer, she grabbed her daughter and rushed upstairs right past me.

Once in a while, I crossed paths with them coming up or down the stairs. The daughter always exchanged a smile with me. As the years went by and she grew up, we never spoke; I didn't even know her name.

In the building I live in, there are many foreign people from South and Central America, Mexico, the Caribbean, and India. They all keep to themselves. It isn't like how it was when I was growing up in Manhattan and all the neighbors knew each other. Back then, we always talked to each other, and all of the children in the building communicated and played with one another.

On a Friday in April of 2008, I was entering my building, and the woman I am speaking of was on her way out. I suddenly felt the urge to take her by the arm and I did. It was like my hand was grabbed by some unseen force; I was being channeled. Channeling is a means of communicating with any consciousness that is not in human form by allowing that consciousness to express itself through the channel, in this case me. As I touched her, I felt immediately that she was very psychic. I was unsure of what kind of reception it would be taken in, if I shared what I was feeling. Some people are skeptics, and depending on their religion, they might take offence; but I decided to tell her anyway. I told her that I felt she was very psychic. I just knew it for some reason, and I sensed that it was an external influence that guided me to tell her. It was as though something wanted to bring us together. She responded by saying, "Yes, I am. How did you know?" I escorted her further into the main lobby, but I had not answered her yet.

I started to pick up on the spirits that were around her; there were several of them. One in particular was her aunt. When her aunt started to appear in my mind's eye, I described her. I told her that her aunt wore East Indian attire; she had very dark hair and wore it pulled to the back like a pony tail. I told her that her aunt's name sounded like it started with "Rad." She told me that her aunt's name was "Radhika." That was when she realized that I was like her. She told me her name. It was an East Indian name, but to protect her privacy, I will call her Elizabeth. I felt that the spirits were very concerned about Elizabeth, especially her aunt Radhika, but I did not yet know why.

Like me, she had been born and raised in New York City. Elizabeth looked like a fashion model. She was five-foot-nine, had long, straight, very black hair to her hips. Her features were very fine with high cheekbones and dark brown eyes; she was striking and was a bit childlike. You could see her East Indian heritage. I briefly told her about how her aunt and other spirits that were around her felt and that they were very concerned for her. We both agreed that the building entrance wasn't the place to discuss this. She wanted to sit and talk, so she invited me to her apartment. She told me that she would be back in about an hour and asked if I could meet her there around that time. I agreed and told her that I would be there.

In that one hour, my excitement grew. I would be around someone like myself. Someone like-minded who would possibly understand me. Unfortunately, I was mistaken; Elizabeth's problems were too much even for me to handle.

When it was time to meet Elizabeth, I walked up to the third floor to her apartment. As I was reaching for her door and before I even touched it, I felt a heaviness. Images of people in my mind's eye started displaying themselves to me; some looked angry, as though they didn't want me to enter her apartment. I sensed that I should be very cautious, or maybe I should just turn around and forget it. I felt that Elizabeth needed help, and so I proceeded and knocked on her door. She opened the door with a smile.

I was greeted and asked to come in. I walked into her apartment and she gestured with her hand for me to sit down.

184

I sat and was overcome with a feeling of uneasiness. The apartment felt overpowering, as though it was shrouded in a thick veil. I felt like I was being suffocated. With my blockage only recently being removed, my abilities were newly reawakened and revealed to me. I wasn't sufficiently experienced to be comfortable about what was happening; I didn't know what to expect next. I knew that Radhika had confidence in me to try to help Elizabeth; it was I who lacked that confidence in myself. The spirit world knows what we can do, even if we don't realize it yet. I asked Elizabeth for a much-needed glass of water. She asked me if I was okay, because she noticed that I looked a bit uncomfortable. I didn't want to frighten her. I told her, "I have to tell you what I am feeling here, and I don't want to alarm you." I explained to her that I felt that her aunt Radhika was worried about her and that she felt that I could help her.

I asked her if she could walk me around her apartment and she agreed. The apartment had two bedrooms, a living room, kitchen, one bathroom, long hallways, and lots of closets; it was much larger than mine. I got up and she led me to her son's bedroom; he didn't live with her anymore. It didn't feel too bad in his room and then we proceeded to the bathroom, again nothing. I asked if I could open up closets, and she agreed. They too felt clear to me. When we walked into the kitchen, I felt a heavy energy there, but I couldn't pinpoint what it was. I can say it felt very grim as it did in the living room.

When we entered her bedroom, I discovered a lot. I felt very negative presences; they weren't virtuous at all. I began to feel pressure on the right side of my head, the spiritual side of my brain. My crown and third-eye chakras started to activate; this was my built-in alarm system that there were heavy spiritual energies present. I asked her, "When you are lying down, do you feel something trying to grab your legs and touching

185

you?" Her answer was, "YES, I DO!"

This thing was perverted and wicked; it was a sexual predator. Suddenly I felt the hairs on my arms and the back of my neck stand on end. When I walked to the right side of her bed, I felt like I walked into a wall of cob webs. It didn't want me there. It was making me feel as though I had to leave because I detected it, and when I closed my eyes, I saw it in my mind's eye. It looked very tall and skinny and was male. He was Caucasian and looked like he had marks on his arms, the kind that someone has who constantly uses syringes. His clothing looked raggedy and dirty, and his teeth looked rotten. There was a foul smell in the room. I felt other nasty spirits in her room as well, but this one was the most powerful.

I contemplated whether this entity was an *incubus*. An incubus is a demon in male form who, according to a number of mythological and legendary traditions, lies upon sleepers, especially women, in order to have sexual intercourse with them. Its female counterpart is the *succubus*. An incubus may pursue sexual relations with a woman in order to father a child, as in the legend of Merlin. Religious tradition holds that repeated intercourse with an incubus or succubus may result in the deterioration of health, or even death.

I didn't feel that this entity was an incubus, but an earthbound spirit. This spirit wasn't very good in physical life and now, in spirit form, was worse. I am not a demonologist, but I know a few. They told me that an incubus demon is very hard to get rid of. Demons are much stronger than earthbound spirits. I felt somewhat relieved because I didn't want to deal with any demons. I had had no experience in doing so.

It was a low-vibrational entity like the one that had once been attached to me. I felt that it had been with Elizabeth for close

186

to a year, and it knew how to conceal itself from her, even though she was a gifted psychic medium. I had firsthand experience that we can be unaware of them. I have learned that Elizabeth had great issues that had attracted low vibrational entities.

I told her that there were low-vibrational entities in her apartment. I explained that one is much stronger than the others, but not a demon. She became very concerned and asked me, "How could this have happened?" I told her that I wasn't sure yet, but that there had to be some explanation. I knew there had to be something that made her vulnerable enough for this thing to attach itself to her, but what? What she was experiencing was the same things I had gone through when I had that dreadful entity attached to me. Similar to what had happened to me, this entity was draining her of her energy.

She always felt tired, had bad headaches, and constantly had nightmares. She couldn't sleep, and when she did sleep, she sometimes woke up finding bruises on her body. As I did, she smelled bad odors like from rotting food and old urine. She said that she heard voices, as though they were having a conversation about her, and she always felt like she was being watched.

We went back into the living room. While I was sitting there with her, I began to see shadows moving about. When I see spirits while giving a mediumship reading, I see them in my mind's eye clearly and describe them to the sitter. When I see spirits with my physical eyes, I don't see them as they looked when they had a body. I see a wisp of a shadow or light, or a transparent mass moving about. If I close my eyes, I might see them, but being a medium and using my other abilities, I can sense if what I am seeing is a male or female. I might also get a name, and if I ask them, they may or may not give me information about themselves.

I was working on devising a plan to get rid of those entities. Mind you, I didn't have much experience in taking on a task such as this, but I had gotten rid of the attachment I had had. It had worked for me, so I wanted to try to help Elizabeth, using the same methods. As I was getting ready to talk with her, we heard her bedroom door slam shut. We were stunned. We got up to go see what had made the door slam and there was no explanation. She told me that had never happened before. It was winter and all of her windows in the apartment were shut and locked. I felt this one particular entity was very angry because it knew that I was going to help Elizabeth. We went back to the living room and sat down.

I was working from a bit of knowledge I had gained from watching paranormal investigative shows on television about debunking. The idea is to expose the falseness or hollowness of a myth, idea, or belief.

"Elizabeth, your aunt Radhika is here for a reason. She is worried about you."

"Why is she worried about me?" She wanted to know.

"She knows that I am a medium and she channeled me to get your attention. Elizabeth, I feel very uncomfortable in this apartment right now and I'm a bit nauseous."

She asked me why I felt so uneasy.

I said: "I didn't know what your aunt wanted from me, but now coming into your apartment I can feel something isn't right here. I am feeling that a very low-vibrational entity is here and it has been with you for some time now. You have been having nightmares, you get cold chills, and you are very depressed. I am also getting that you have thoughts of suicide and nothing seems to go right for you; you wake up with bruises sometimes." (Although I mentioned the bruises earlier, they were unknown to me at the time.) I then very carefully brought this to her attention.

At that very moment, as I was telling her this, I got goose bumps all over and felt a chill. I knew that the entity didn't like that I was warning Elizabeth about it.

I feel that one of the reasons God gave me these gifts is to help those who are going through what Elizabeth was suffering, and I had personal experience with my own attachment. God gave me the gift of discernment for a reason, and I must use it. I shared some of my own experiences and told Elizabeth that I succeeded in ridding myself of the low-vibrational entity that had attached itself to me. That had been my only direct experience with such a thing.

I told her that I could come back on Saturday with some tools to try to free her from those entities, but that she would have to be an active participant. This was her apartment and she needed to reclaim it from her attached entity along with the other lower-vibrational entities that were there. When it's someone else's home, those who live in it have to take charge, but I told her I would be there for support. At that point, I had to leave the apartment. I was feeling tired and my energy had been drained. I reassured Elizabeth and told her that everything would be fine.

The Cleansing

I am a Spiritualist Christian, and when I go about clearing and cleansing my space with prayer, sage smudging, and spraying, I ask Jesus Christ to be present and remove anything malevolent that doesn't belong in our home, anything that

189

works against us. When I help people now, I go by whatever religion they practice and I ask them to deliver their prayers. I know that there is only one God, but some religions might use a different name for the same God. God is pure Universal Love.

Saturday came and I began to gather what I needed. I had smudge sage, a spray bottle of blessed sea-salt water, and a large brass cross.

Smudge sage was originally used by Native American Indians and shamans. It is a bundle of dry white sage tied together with string and when burned, the fragrances facilitate spiritual cleansing. It clears negative energy or entities, creates harmony, and it is used in meditation and for medicinal purposes.

I walked up to Elizabeth's apartment at about 1 p.m. She opened the door, but this time she didn't have a smile on her face. I asked her if she was okay.

She said, "Since that day you came here, things have been weird. Objects have been moving about, and while I am lying down, I keep hearing a voice telling me not to let you do what you're planning on doing."

I told her, "That doesn't surprise me, Elizabeth. They want to keep the hold they have on you. You have to be strong." I felt that she had gone through more than she had told me, but it wasn't from the spirits.

"Elizabeth, what religion do you practice, or do you practice any at all?" She said that she was Christian. I was surprised that she was also a Christian. That made it easier for me. At the time, I was not aware that Christianity was India's third-largest religion.

"I have brought some tools with me that will be very helpful in trying to get rid of the problem here." I was thinking to myself, *I hope I know what I am doing. This is my second cleansing, including my own.* Elizabeth was a chain smoker; I asked her not to smoke while this was being done.

I brought a large abalone shell with me. Abalone shell is a colorful shell that incorporates the beautiful colors of the sea. It has its own metaphysical and healing properties. Like other sources of vibrational healing from Nature, abalone shells have a strong elemental bond with the Earth and its healing capabilities. I placed pieces of dried sage onto the shell.

I began to give Elizabeth instructions on how we would and should proceed with the cleansing. I had found a house cleansing prayer that I had used for myself and now use all the time to cleanse my apartment. I printed it out and brought it with me so she could recite it.

"Here is the house cleansing prayer." I handed the paper to her and I had a copy for myself. "I will light the sage, and we will start at your son's room, and the prayer will have to be said in every room we go into. You will have to be stern and loud and you must mean it. This is your home and you must be the one to say it and take charge of your environment and your life."

She looked a bit nervous, but then she said ,"I am ready, let's do it!" Before we started, I grabbed the spray bottle of blessed sea-salt water and sprayed it on both of us from head to toe. I carried the brass cross in my hand.

I lit the sage and we walked into her son's room. The sage started to billow up all around. I asked Elizabeth to start the prayer.

"By the blood of Jesus Christ, I bind every evil spirit that is in this room and command them to flee right now and go where the Lord Jesus Christ sends them. I renounce and reject any inch of this house and property that has been yielded or surrendered unto Satan and by faith I take it back and surrender it to the Lord Jesus Christ. By faith, I claim that this room is covered under the blood of the Lord Jesus Christ and no evil spirit can enter it."

We opened every closet and said the prayer in every room, including the bathroom. We finally got to her bedroom. On our way there, we felt heavy like we were being pushed back, but the sage kept neutralizing any negative energies that were in our way. We entered her bedroom. This was the room where the entity was felt the strongest; it was very angry. The hairs on my arms and neck stood up and the stench of old urine was very strong. My crown and third-eye chakras were now being activated very violently; I was seeing transparent masses moving about.

Again Elizabeth started to recite the prayer; this time, she was much louder and very serious. She put her foot down in a powerful way. That was what was needed because it started to feel much lighter in the room. I started to pray for a powerful warrior archangel to come in: "Archangel Michael, we ask for your divine protection. Please spread your beautiful violet web of light all over this apartment and remove all that is malevolent." I closed my eyes and saw flashes of light, beautiful swirls of light. The apartment was feeling clearer and clearer and my chakras were calming down, which was a good sign.

After we finished and the sage smoke had dissipated, Elizabeth told me that she felt like she was going to throw up while she was reciting the prayer. I told her that I had felt that way, too, when I got rid of my attachment. It had been attached to her aura and when it left, she was affected that way. "I feel so clear now," she said.

I reminded her that she must continue to protect herself and live a healthier lifestyle. She would have to learn to manage her gifts as well.

We opened some windows so the apartment could air out and we sat down in the living room. The feeling of the apartment had totally changed. The negative veil I felt when I had first entered the apartment had lifted. There was something about Elizabeth, though. Although the negative entities had departed, there remained a darkness about her. I felt that there was a reason that all of the negative energy had clung to her.

While sitting there, I suggested that we could help each other. I wanted to do psychic development and since she was gifted, I felt that we could get some books and do some exercises. She needed someone to try to stabilize her, and I felt that I could help her in that. "I don't have much experience myself, Elizabeth, but we can start out and see what happens." She agreed and was very eager to get started.

At first it was going well. She would sometimes come up to my apartment to do chakra humming, and my mother thought we were two nuts. We were lying on the floor with crystals on top of us and humming a different mantra for each of the chakra centers; there are seven main chakras. We also meditated, mostly visualizing. This is great for strengthening clairvoyance.

Once I was up in her apartment and we were getting ready to do a psychic exercise using cards. We used regular playing cards and we shuffled the cards and split the deck. She would get one half and I the other. We were sitting on the floor facing each other. Each of us would place 10 cards in front of us facing down. The object of the exercise was to psychically get the suit of each card and turn the card over to see if we were accurate or not. Once I got 9 out of 10 correct; that was considered excellent. Elizabeth had a huge ego and would get upset when she didn't do well.

At one point I looked up to observe her, and behind her I saw a man. He looked East Indian and had on a turban. He didn't look very happy. "Elizabeth, don't be alarmed, but there is man behind you."

She turned around and said, "I don't see anyone." She was more of a psychic than a medium.

"I am seeing him in my mind's eye," I told her. "He is saying his name to me, but I don't know if I've got it right or not. He is saying Paksha."

She said, "Oh my God, that is my father's name."

I have always had a knack for getting names. "He is wearing a turban and has a mustache," I told her.

"Yes that is correct." She was eager to validate the information.

"I am feeling that he had a massive heart attack and he also had a blood issue like diabetes."

She answered this sadly, "Yes, he was found by my stepmother in their apartment hallway. He had suffered a heart attack and yes, he had diabetes and some other issues as well."

"Elizabeth, he doesn't seem very happy to me for some reason. He is worried about you and it has to do with something that happened to you." I wasn't feeling that it had to do with the negative spirits that we evicted from her apartment; it was something much worse.

194

Elizabeth began to cry and told me that she knew why he was there. I felt that it wasn't any of my business and I didn't ask her. She decided to tell me herself, and it left me shocked. I remember feeling something dark about her, and I knew right then and there this was it.

She told her father that she loved him; she was happy that he had come to pay her a visit.

He told her, through me, that he always came to visit her. Since I was able to see him, it was the perfect time for him to try to get a message to her. That message was, "Let it pass and move on with your life."

She again began to sob and he slowly faded out of my mind's eye.

She was a bit nervous and hesitated to speak. "One year ago, I was coming home on a Saturday night at about 2:45 a.m." She placed the palms of her hands on her face and paused. "I was drinking and was a bit out of it, but I wasn't extremely drunk."

I felt a rush of energy hit me; a feeling of complete dread came over me. My empathic ability picked up on how she was feeling.

"I got to the front of the building and opened the door. I was moving fast not noticing anything behind me. I should have looked back, but I didn't."

Again, I felt what she was feeling.

"I walked up to my apartment here and put in my key. As I was opening the door, I felt a hand grab my mouth, stopping me from screaming. I froze and I was pushed into my apartment. I was taken into my bedroom. There were three men, but they were wearing dark shades and I couldn't fully

195

see their faces.

One of them took out a syringe and stuck it into my arm. I suddenly felt immobilized, I couldn't move; they had given me some kind of a drug."

At this point, I didn't know what to say, but worse was about to come.

"They raped me, one after the other. That is all I remember. I woke up on my bed and I was afraid to get up. I thought that they were still in my apartment. When I did get up, I went all around checking to see if anyone was there, but they were gone. They took several of my belongings and some money I had in my pocketbook. I called the police, and they immediately took me to the hospital to have me checked out and took semen samples. Later they interviewed me for the report."

"I am sorry this happened to you, Elizabeth." I didn't really know what to say; I was still shocked. I didn't understand why this would happen in our building, with a police precinct right at the corner. Those men must have been watching her, because somehow they knew that she lived by herself. I noticed that the security in the building had been beefed up a lot with cameras all over; there weren't any before. Now I understood. This is what I had been feeling about her, but couldn't quite sort out.

Throughout the following months, as I saw and got together with Elizabeth, she always looked confused and troubled. She continuously spoke of how she felt that people were out to get her. She became obsessed with keeping her apartment clear of negativity. She seemed to be constantly smudging her apartment with sage and praying intensely. She became fearful of the spirits and people around her. She thought that neighbors were working some negative spiritual spells on her.

She was also afraid to leave her apartment. Mentally she kept slipping into this other place where no one could reach her. Her therapy wasn't having much effect. She lost a lot of weight, and her once beautiful looks were fading; she looked physically ill. She developed a phobia of being touched, especially by men.

Elizabeth couldn't cope at all, she was seeing a psychiatrist, and since she couldn't work, she was on disability. She was also taking psychotropic medication. As the months went by, I noticed that she would talk about people putting negative spells on her. She was convinced that her stepmother was after her and that she was working some hoodoo on her.

Hoodoo is also known as "conjure" and sometimes confused with "voodoo." It is a traditional African-American folk spiritual practice that developed from a number of West African, Native American, and European spiritual traditions.

I don't know if Elizabeth was imagining all of that, but I do know that it does exist. Throughout the months, her condition worsened. I also felt that she was taking illegal drugs to help her cope, because many times when I saw her, she was incoherent. All of this was due to the rape, of course. It was all very sad. She was out of control.

I now understand why Elizabeth attracted negative energies to herself. She was a perfect candidate for them. One day I ran into her in the hallway and I stopped to talk with her. She told me that she was going to move to Florida to stay with her mother; she left a month later. I haven't seen or heard from her since. I hope she is doing better and I do include her in my prayers.

The negative spirits that were in Elizabeth's apartment weren't nearly as bad as the human beings that did what they did to her.

197

Chapter Nine

My Dear Louise

"Make yourself familiar with the angels and behold
them frequently in spirit; for without being seen,
they are present with you." — *St. Francis De Sales*

In 2009, while I was still involved in a spiritual forum and
giving tarot card readings, I was helping a woman we shall
call "Samantha" to locate a misplaced watch. During this
reading, I felt another presence around me — a presence that
I can only describe as feminine and loving. I turned to
Andreas and said, "Andreas, I know that the information I
just gave to this woman was being given to me clairaudiently.
I felt a female presence and I could hear her speaking to me;
she was conveying messages."

Clairaudience is another form of extrasensory perception. It is
when a person acquires information through paranormal
auditory sources. It is often considered to be a form of
clairvoyance, but it is essentially the ability to hear in a
paranormal manner. While clairvoyance is to see,
clairsentience is to feel.

Clairaudience may refer not to actual perception of sound,
but may instead indicate impressions in the mind similar to
the way many people think words without having auditory
impressions. But it may also refer to actual perception of
sound, such as voices, tones, or noises that are not apparent
to other humans or to recording equipment. For instance, a
clairaudient person may hear the voices or thoughts of spirits.

Sometimes after I had gone to bed, I would hear my name

199

being shouted out: "FREDDIE!" or "MISTER RIVERA!" and a whole lot of other ruckus and comments I don't care to repeat. They weren't all yelling. Some would come in softly, but only when I was lying down and completely relaxed. Now it happens at any given time and I just shrug it off as someone trying to get my attention. Some people might consider themselves schizophrenic or may even be misdiagnosed with it, but I didn't even contemplate that idea.

One time I was getting ready to meditate and I was in the mood to do it lying down. I placed a quilt on the floor with a small pillow; it was in July and it was very hot that day. I didn't have an air conditioner in the living room, just a tall fan that oscillated. I decided to tilt the fan towards me on the floor, by placing a book under its legs. When I got the fan just the way I wanted it, I lay down on the quilt facing up with my arms to my sides. I began to meditate. About ten minutes into the meditation, I heard "FREDDIE!" and two seconds later the fan came crashing to the floor. It was completely destroyed; the blades and a few of its legs were broken. I got up very quickly and unplugged it. I was very upset because the fan was an expensive one and now I didn't have a way to keep cool.

It occurred to me that I had received a warning beforehand, but only by about two seconds. It wouldn't have made any difference anyway. Back then I wouldn't have figured out that it was a warning. Even if the voice had told me, "Freddie the fan is going to fall," instead of just shouting "FREDDIE!," I don't think I would have had time to stop the fan from falling. A few medium friends of mine have told me that they, too, have received warnings. Some were driving and, because they paid attention to the warning, they avoided catastrophes.

That winter, my mother's room wasn't getting enough heat, so we purchased an electric heater. One evening after going to bed with the heater on, I was suddenly awakened by my mother's screams. "FREDDIE, FREDDIE!" It was about two thirty in the morning and I sprang to my feet and ran to my mother's room. There was smoke everywhere, and I saw that a box was in flames. I didn't even think, I just grabbed the box and ran to the bathroom with it. I tossed the box into the bathtub and turned on the shower until the fire was completely extinguished. I went back to my mother's room and held her; she was shaking and so was I.

Once I had calmed her down, she told me, "You called out to me twice; I heard your voice yelling MA, MA! It woke me up and I turned over on the bed and noticed the fire. This is when I yelled out to you."

I told her "Ma, I didn't call out to you. I was asleep."

She said, "I heard you." My mother, being clairaudient herself, heard the warning from the other side. We are surely protected and loved.

I cleaned everything up. After my mother was calmed and back in her bed, I went back to my own bed and started to cry. I can just imagine what would have happened if my mother hadn't received that warning. I thanked God for our safety and finally was able to fall asleep again.

Ever since Samantha's reading I had been wondering: *Who was that female entity giving me information during that reading?* When I looked for answers from Andreas, I heard him say telepathically: "You will soon know." Andreas never gives me information in that manner; I always feel what he wants to convey to me in an empathic way. For some reason, he felt that he had to relay this to me in another manner. I was excited that I would soon find out whose angelic voice that had been. I suspected it was the same voice that had warned me about the fan. I remained alert; I didn't want to miss it.

Regardless, she would know the right moment to introduce herself.

For two weeks after I questioned Andreas about the female entity, I heard nothing more. At last one morning I felt an energy around me. At first I thought it was Andreas, but I soon realized that I was mistaken. Around noon I went to do some errands for my mother at the grocery store. While I was there, I still felt the energy. I knew that it wasn't Andreas because his energy feels different than this new one. All of my spirit guides emanate what I would call signature energies. Andreas emanates a more direct, stronger energy — more like a male energy. The one I was feeling around me that day felt softer, more feminine. I just shrugged it off for the time being and kept shopping.

After I got back home and was talking with my mother while putting the groceries away, I suddenly became a bit faint. I felt guided to go into the living room. As I entered, I had to do a double take; I could not believe what I was seeing. There was a beautiful woman standing next to Andreas; it was the first time I saw Andreas standing up instead of squatting down on one knee. The woman smiled a very warm smile at me; she seemed utterly serene. I felt a need to sit down. I slowly took a seat on the couch, still facing them both. She began speaking to me telepathically. "Hello Freddie, I am Louise," she said. "I am here to help you."

Louise radiated a pinkish and white glow; she wore garments like those I have seen women wear in Arabian movies. Her headdress reminded me of the Virgin Mary. Louise was transparent like Andreas. I thought I was seeing an angel, but Louise is another spirit guide. I have a wing chair in my living room and I asked her to please sit down. The wing chair is very special to me and I was honored that she agreed to sit down on it. After she sat down, Andreas swiftly squatted down again.

Not knowing what to do or say, I just sat there staring at her. Finally I turned to look at Andreas. I felt as though I was in the twilight zone. I had heard her voice before, during my reading with Samantha. It was the same voice, but now the image belonging to it was right in front of me.

Louise just sat there on the wing chair with a loving and peaceful look on her face. I thought to myself, *what now?*

My mother startled me. She came into the room asking: "What are you doing, why are you talking to yourself?"

I told her that I was just thinking out loud. I hadn't realized that I was communicating with my voice. I changed to communicating telepathically. Andreas and Louise were pleased that I discovered how to deal with this. It wouldn't do for people to think that I was going out of my mind! Communicating in this manner took a little getting used to, but now it's a part of me. It is like second nature. However, I still use my voice when I am alone.

I began to feel self-conscious about my thoughts. *Oh my God, they heard that!* and I also felt like I had lost my privacy. I even started to get dressed in the bathroom instead of in my room. When I would take a shower, I wondered if they were in there with me. Were they around during other intimate moments?

I brought this up on a post in the forum. A member responded to my post by saying, "Freddie, they have been with you all of your life and there is nothing they don't know about you. I felt the same way you did at first, but then I thought: hey, they already know everything about me. I really didn't care anymore." After thinking about what the forum member said, I began to feel a little foolish.

My spirit guides have a full understanding of how I feel. They have reincarnated many times as physical beings themselves. When it was time, they chose not to reincarnate again. They had already learned all they wanted to learn from each of their previous lives. I stopped worrying and continued living my life as before. I did pay more attention to the way I thought; that was very hard to do and still is.

I wondered if what I was experiencing was common among sensitive people. It made me uncomfortable to think that I was somehow different; that I was the only one who was able to see and communicate with my guides. I went on the forum and wrote a post. "Have you physically seen your spirit guides?"

I waited a couple of days for a reply. When I looked, I was amazed at the number of responses my post had generated: "Yes I have seen my guides." "I have seen my protector spirit guide." "My gatekeeper guide is with me right now." There were countless other responses. People wrote about and shared their experiences. Wow, I was so happy that I was not the only one. But why *would* I be the only one? After all, everyone on this planet has a team of spirit guides, but not everyone knows about them. One woman wrote that she thought she was going crazy. I thought about it and whispered to myself, "Just like I did." And I concluded that I was not. How could I have helped Samantha find her watch if I didn't have any help?

I remembered reading a book about a spirit guide that gives the medium information about the sitter clairaudiantly. I recalled hearing her when I was reading Samantha and I understood Louise to have done that for me. I later found out that she was my gatekeeper and mediumship development spirit guide as well.

A very gifted psychic medium told me, after I met Louise:

"Freddie, you knew Louise in the afterlife; you chose her to be one of your spirit guides. You two are actually very good friends." I felt the connection instantly and knew it to be true. Louise has been with me ever since I reincarnated back to this earth plane. I chose to learn and experience another life and I knew her before that. It thrilled me that the medium validated this for me.

Louise stands by me while I am reading; I tell her the name and birth date of the person that I am going to read for beforehand. Louise already knows all of that before it even happens, so I know that it's not even necessary. Spirit guides know everything before it happens. They have the ability to know the future; time doesn't exist for them. We humans are linear creatures; we are governed by time, while spirit guides are not.

Developing a relationship with Spirit is very important. In order to be a successful medium, you cannot doubt your abilities. You must have full trust in Spirit and be thankful every day for what God has given you.

God gave all of us wonderful abilities as human beings; we are all wired the same. Many people have no idea about what they are capable of, but they have the capacities just the same.

I am deeply grateful for the gifts God has given me. I am not the Freddie I used to be; I know that I have awakened from a false reality. Just think about the movie *The Matrix*, when the lead character finds out that the reality he is living in is a computer-generated reality run by artificial intelligence.

One's perception of life and of spirituality is everything. I was not originally a spiritual man. The events and experiences I have related above have awakened me from my unconscious state and led me to embrace my gifts. They have molded me into the person I am today. All of the words at my command are insufficient to fully express the wonder and gratitude that fill my life every minute of every day.

Learning How to Make
Sense of It All

A natural medium is born with their abilities strongly turned on, but even if we are born a natural medium, we still have to learn how to make sense of what we are receiving. We must put the pieces together; information is coming from the other side in different ways. If we pick up information by clairaudient means, for instance, most of the time we don't hear what is being told to us in full sentences. Clairvoyantly, we will see images or little movies in our heads, but what do they mean? We might have to ask the sitter for help. They usually know exactly what these sounds or images mean. Clairsentience is probably the psychic ability that is most difficult to understand because we must gather information with all of our senses to get what the communicator is trying to convey.

I have read many books written by famous psychic mediums. Many of them write about how they began to develop their gift. All of these mediums are natural psychic mediums, as I am. They became a member of a mediumship development circle. One person spent seven years developing his gift before he ever charged to give a reading. He is very gifted, as I have witnessed.

In April of 2008, I decided that I wanted to find and join a mediumship development circle. I wanted to go to an actual circle, where we would be sitting in a circle, learning and practicing. I didn't want to use online development anymore. That method of development had become boring for me. I wanted to get out to meet other like-minded people face to face. I searched and searched until I came across a website called meetup.com. As always, my prayers were answered.

On the site, I did a search for mediumship development within a 20-mile radius of where I lived. I found several meet-ups related to my query. I noticed one in particular: "Psychic and Mediumship Development Circles" offered in downtown Manhattan. I read the description of the meet-up and immediately clicked on "Join." I filled out a questionnaire and I was in; I was now a member of that group.

It is advisable to first "tune up" your psychic abilities before moving on to mediumship, because we use our psychic abilities to gather information from the other side. We have to find out what psychic ability is strongest within us. In my case, I feel that clairsentience is my strongest psychic ability, and clairaudience is my second.

In May of 2008, I decided to attend my first circle on psychic development. Being around other people like myself would be new for me. I didn't know what I might feel from them; I was a bit nervous. When I walked in, a woman by the name of Lee greeted me. I told her my name is Freddie. She said "Hello, Freedy." She had an accent I wasn't used to hearing. She welcomed me with open arms. Lee Van Zyl is a very tall White South African, and a psychic medium and healer. She looked like a force of nature to me, a bit intimidating. Soon that feeling went away. Lee is one of the kindest people I have ever met. When Lee holds a mediumship circle, she is, of course, the circle leader. She is a full-time teaching medium now.

Lee is co-owner of one of the largest metaphysical centers in New Jersey called Montclair Metaphysical. She used to rent space in Manhattan to hold special circles for a number of weeks, in addition to her center in New Jersey. Manhattan is where I first met Lee. She is a lawyer by profession, but she decided to leave her vocation to put all her time into running the center. She is a person who loves teaching and Spirit. She would rather be at the center than anywhere else.

I always wanted to get names when giving a mediumship reading. I can still hear Lee shout at me, "Move on Freddie, forget about the name and move on!"

I don't join in the circles anymore. If I tell Lee I want to go in and join a circle, she tells me, "Freddie, you don't need to be here, you are too advanced." I do like to get away and visit Lee once in a while and to see if any of my friends are at the center. Sometimes I make up any excuse to go there.

Lee Van Zyl – Teaching Medium
Rutherford, New Jersey
http://www.leevanzylpsychicmedium.com
http://www.montclairmetaphysical.com

Freddie Rivera by Lee Van Zyl

I have known Freddie for six years. I first met him in Manhattan when I moved into the area, and started teaching people how to develop their mediumistic abilities. Freddie was one of my first students in this group and through the years has been a great supporter of his fellow mediums as well as my school for mediumistic development.

What stood out about Freddie from the very beginning was his dedication to and his love of the Spirit World. It was quite apparent that Freddie was not merely dabbling, but that he was a natural medium who always seeks to better himself and

209

has subsequently enhanced his abilities by attending various trainings and availing himself to people, and to read without charge very often, so that people can heal and be reunited with their family and friends in Spirit.

The key to the development of a medium is consistency, dedication, a love of our fellow human beings and a love of those who have crossed over to the other side as well as our spirit helpers. This is where Freddie stood out from the others. Where many of the mediums would look for excuses not to attend, Freddie was always at his development circle, on time, no matter what the weather or time. I remember that during some of the circles, it would only be myself and Freddie. He would take trains and several buses from Queens New York to New Jersey where I was teaching at the time, and where now I own and run my own Metaphysical center. It was never easy for him, as he had to also arrange for a caretaker for his elderly mother, so that he could attend a development circle.

Freddie's tenacity and dedication have paid off handsomely and the spirit world has rewarded him with a strong gift of mediumship. Today he continues to work professionally as a medium, not always charging though, and he has dedicated his life to helping people connect with their Loved Ones in Spirit.

It is sometimes a lonely job being a medium. It requires a good healthy lifestyle, the ability to stay focused and positive, no matter what people might say about you, and to always remember why you are doing the work. Freddie has all of these qualities.

I have also learned a lot from Freddie through the years and value his friendship. He is a great mentor for people and a healer with a kind compassionate heart. It is my privilege and honor to say a few words about him – Freddie, Spiritual Medium.

Thanks Freddie for sharing your gifts with us and I wish you many blessings and encouragement on your ongoing journey.

Giving Back — Voice of Our Angels

Giving Back

"Do not judge the bereaved mother. She comes in many forms
She is breathing, but she is dying. She may look young, but
inside she has become ancient. She smiles, but her heart
sobs. She walks, she talks, she cooks, she cleans, she works,
she IS, but she is not, all at once. She is here, but part of her is
elsewhere for eternity." - *Author unknown*

I am always so very thankful to God for the gifts that allow me to help those in need – gifts that are bestowed on all of God's children. I am fortunate that my life's path has led me to recognize and develop abilities that anyone may have with sufficient application and perseverance.

I am sometimes asked the question, "God gave you your gift to help people. Do you think it's a good idea to charge to help people; isn't that wrong?" My answer is no, it's not wrong. We all have and develop different gifts in life. Some pursue their gifts as musicians, painters, writers, scientists, and so on. They charge for what God has given them, just as I do. The other side knows that we as human beings need to survive; we need to make a living somehow, and this is how I make my living now – and I make a difference in people's lives.

I believe that if I take, I must give back in some way. I give back by using *mediumship*. Mediumship is my means of

213

bringing healing to the hearts and minds of those who are grieving deeply from the loss of a loved one; the resulting relief immediate. It is immediate because their loved ones come through with evidence the sitter validates as accurate and messages they fully understand. It's that simple.

I give free readings, but I don't like to give them to those who are merely curious. I would rather give them to individuals who truly need the peace a reading can bring them.

Reading for the members of an organized group is ideal for me, because the group's organizer or leader handles the list of sitters. I contact one proposed sitter at a time from the list, knowing beforehand when I will have free time, and set up a reading date and time with them.

One such group is called "Voice of Our Angels" founded and headed by Ann Marie Martin. Ann Marie lost her son AJ when he was 21 years of age. Wanting to help other parents who have lost a child, she instituted the support group. I commend her for starting it; a lot of the parents are doing so much better because of it. Thank you, Ann Marie!

Ann Marie Martin
Orion, Minnesota
http://www.voiceofourangels.com

Voice of Our Angels

After the devastating loss of my son AJ, at the age of 21, I knew there had to be a way to move from tragedy to just plain functioning. I felt that the answer lies in continuing your relationship with your child even though they are on the other side. I have contact with my son here and there as he leaves signs for me, an occasional MOM in my ear or an I love you, strategically placed feathers and coins and the usual dreams. I felt that the answer to this thing called grief was in receiving that message from spirit. I know how it provided healing for me after my first reading.

I met Freddie through Divine Intervention, I am convinced. I don't remember through whom but he has been a GODSEND! My name is Ann Marie and I am founder of Voice of Our Angels Support Group for grieving parents. This group enables parents to once again communicate as they always had through wonderful and talented mediums like Freddie. My son prompted me to form this group so he can gather the children on the other side, while the parents gather on earth to receive their child's love once again. He gives of his time and offers each and every one of our parents a free half hour reading to prove that these kids go on.

You see, Freddie provides the evidence that life does go on. There is so much healing that occurs after these readings! A parent who was unable to get dressed, go out or even be social with others, all of a sudden now has joy again. The change is immediate and everlasting. I have seen parent after parent "snap" out of it because of the messages they receive

215

from Freddie. Many times there is resolution to the circumstances around the death that plagued the parent and kept them stuck, worried and unable to function. Sometimes the child provides that through the message. When they hear a loving, "Hi Mom" or "I love you" it lifts the spirit and calms the soul to a once broken heart unlike anything! Our group is so grateful to Freddie to his devotion to healing the broken heart by delivering a message. Quite a few of our members have told me that Freddie has saved their life! For that... I am grateful.

A Life Saving Reading

I have been working as a professional psychic medium for over six years now, but I have been who I am all of my life. A mediumship reading gives closure and healing to those who have lost a loved one. The reading also extends out to their families, so the reading keeps healing. There are times when a mediumship reading reaches out and saves lives. This particular visit from heaven did just that; after this reading, I know why I have this extraordinary gift.

I am not a necromancer; I don't call spirits to me. It's astonishing how the spirits know that their loved ones here on this earth plane are going to have a reading. Most of the time, they show up.

I have many private clients, and I also work for an online psychic reading company. The company is based on chat readings first; I can also give phone readings if the client wishes it. As a rule, I do not give mediumship readings through chat; it just doesn't work. The vibration is high and information comes in fast. I usually need quick validation. Chat just doesn't do mediumship readings justice. I feel it is disrespectful to the spirits.

I was recommended by one of my other clients to a woman who wanted a mediumship reading. I will call her Claire. Claire sent an e-mail to me on the service where I do readings asking for a mediumship reading. I responded with dates and times when I was available. We set a date and time.

217

Before the reading, Louise made me feel that this reading was going to be different. Louise stands by me when I am giving mediumship readings. I don't like to tune in beforehand when I am going to give a reading; it all has to happen right then and there while the reading is in progress. I specifically do not want to know anything from the client about loved ones on the other side. I must be objective and not influenced by the sitter's information or expectations. Prior information can taint evidence that I should pick up on my own from the loved one that is coming through.

Claire seemed a bit nervous when she called on time for our appointment. I tried to make her feel more comfortable. I always ask my clients if they are sitting up comfortably and if they have something to write with in case they want to take notes. Before I begin the reading, I say a short prayer and ask if they would like me to do a medical intuitive scan on them afterwards. She decided she didn't want one. Since it was a telephone reading, I advised her that if she hears me talking to someone, I am not talking to a physical person. I am talking to my spirit guides or to the loved ones that are coming through.

I work with gathering evidence from the other side before I ask for the messages the spirit wants to communicate to the sitter. A communicator is the spirit that is coming through. First, I ask for the name of the communicator. Next, I ask if I can see them. I focus on sensing and understanding their personality. I ask how their physical body died and their relationship to the sitter. I want to know the communicator's age when they crossed over. The communicator has to prove to me and to the sitter that they are who they say they are by providing these verifiable pieces of evidence. If I get four pieces of evidence, I will be content to begin the reading.

I told Claire, "I am feeling a presence, a male one. I am getting a V name and it sounds like Vincent to me."

Gasping and breathing heavily, Claire replied: "Yes, that is my son, Vincent."

"He is showing himself to me, Claire. He is tall, has short dark brown hair and light skin. He looks to me like he is 21 to 25 years old and he is wearing what looks like a baseball jersey."

"Oh yes, he loved baseball and played on a team. You described him exactly."

"I am hearing March, the month." I told her.

I can show compassion more easily during an in-person reading. It's more difficult over the telephone. I have to reach out somehow to comfort the sitter while maintaining my objectivity as best I can. After her son Vincent mentioned March, Claire broke down and started to cry uncontrollably. It took a little time before she was ready to continue with the reading.

When she could speak of it, she said: "That is the month he died."

"I am feeling like I am in a car. This wasn't a natural death, it was a car accident."

"Yes, he was a passenger in the front seat."

"I am getting the driver was drunk."

"Yes, his friend was drinking."

"I feel a head injury and pain on my chest."

"The other car hit the car on the side my son was sitting on – the right side. They said the other car was going 60 miles an hour. My son was killed instantly; his head and chest were crushed."

"Yes, I feel that he crossed over immediately. Claire, he is saying that he didn't suffer; he didn't feel anything. He is saying that he was pulled out of his body before the crash and that two family members were there waiting for him. He followed them into a beautiful white light."

Again Claire broke down and then said to her son, "I am so happy that you didn't suffer."

Vincent suddenly became agitated; he was rushing, trying to get my attention. I remembered Louise's warning. I realized that it had to do with how Vincent was acting.

I heard the words "She is planning..." he gave it to me a few words at a time because he didn't want me to miss his message. "...to kill herself," he went on. The information was starting to make sense to me. "Commit suicide..." I suddenly became concerned. "...because of my death," he said.

Now I had the whole picture. Claire was planning to commit suicide because of Vincent's death; she couldn't deal with not having her son with her. "Please stop her!" He was pleading with me to tell her that he knew what she was planning, in hopes that she would not do it. I told him, "I will, Vincent."

This was a delicate situation. I had to pass along Vincent's message in a way that would have the desired impact on Claire. "Claire, Vincent loves you very much. He is telling me that you are a wonderful mother. He says that he comes around you to check up on you. He is saying that he isn't dead, but has gone home to God. It was his time."

Claire interrupted me. "But why! He was so young; he had a whole life ahead of him!" She was crying.

This is one reading when I wish I was there in person, I thought to myself.

"Claire, Vincent wants you to know something," I continued. "He has told me that you are planning on taking your own life because of his death."

She broke down crying uncontrollably again. I was shaken. *Oh my Lord!* I thought.

When she was again calm enough to proceed, I continued giving the message. That was what Vincent wanted me to do. "He is saying that he doesn't want you to do that; it's not your time to go home to God yet. He is saying that you and he will see and be with each other again when it's time for you to cross over, but that time isn't now."

I was asking God mentally while the message was being given "God, please help me. Let Vincent's message to his mother heal her. Let her realize that taking her own life isn't the answer."

My prayer was answered.

Suddenly Claire became calm and serene; I could sense a new lightness in her spirit, as if a ton of bricks had lifted off her chest.

She said, "Thank you Freddie. I am glad that I had this reading with you. Now when I want to talk to my son, I will come to you."

I told her, "You can always talk to Vincent without me. All you have to do is think of him and he will be there, always."

Claire breathed. "Thank you Vincent, again you have made me proud to be your mother. I miss you and wish every day that you were here with me, but now I know that you are fine. I now know that death is not the end and I will see you again someday. I don't want to ever disappoint you, Vincent, and I will do as you wish. You have saved me, my son and I love you with all of my heart."

Claire thanked me, and the reading ended. Was this a coincidence? No, it wasn't; I don't believe in coincidences. This reading was meant to be given, because it had a powerful message to deliver and a life-saving mission.

I communicated with Claire about a month afterwards. She immediately let me know that she was fine. The reading had been life-changing for her and healed her in more ways than she could express. She also said that whenever she thinks about Vincent, she immediately feels his presence and his love.

Chapter Ten
Proof Positive

'... when you have eliminated the impossible, whatever
remains, *however improbable*, must be the truth...'
- *Sir Arthur Conan Doyle* creator of Sherlock Holmes

In this last chapter of my book I wanted to show you how
mediumship can be used to help heal the mind and the heart
– and that the results can be instant. I don't want you to feel
that I am claiming that what I do is better than the services of
a mental health specialist. I have a lot of respect for what they
do. A reading by a good medium can provide critical
information and insights that help resolve difficult problems.
Such a reading can support many forms of therapy. I always
stress to everyone that they should do their homework when
looking for a reputable psychic medium.

When I have any issue that needs addressing, I look for a
person with a good track record specializing in that field.
Usually for me, that information comes from word of mouth.
As I have mentioned before, I am an "evidential medium." I
must give at least four to five pieces of evidence to the sitter,
that they can validate, that the person coming through is who
they say they are. The messages I relay must make sense. If
this is accomplished successfully from the beginning of the
reading, the healing can take place in a very powerful way.
This is always my goal and what drives me to do this work.

This book was written to serve a purpose. That is to prove
that the consciousness survives after the physical body has
died and to show the healing benefits of mediumship. I give

readings to a wide range of individuals. No matter what our status in life, we all experience the need to heal from a loss or losses. I have added testimonials written by authors, lawyers, and other professional people, along with housewives and the everyday average person. These people wanted to share how a mediumship reading has changed or saved their own life. I asked the editors to do very minimal work, so that these testimonials are in each individual's own words.

I have added a little of the personal information (with permission of course) of the people who have written their testimonials, for authenticity. It is my hope that with this added credibility, more people will feel comfortable and open to experiencing a reading and healing of their own. I read for people all over the world and I give the readings by telephone. Readings are relaxed and done in the comfort of the person's own home.

Spirit never ceases to amaze me. I still often feel as if I were experiencing the powerful way they can communicate for the very first time. I hope these testimonials bring you comfort in knowing that we don't die; love continues on.

Simone Gabbay
Toronto, ON Canada
simonegabbay.com

Simone is the author of three books based on the readings of the late Christian mystic and visionary Edgar Cayce.

Freddie Rivera: A Direct Link to Heaven

Even if we believe that consciousness survives death, as some 80 percent of North Americans do, the death of a loved one is extremely difficult to come to terms with. One of the hardest aspects of losing someone close to us is that we can no longer communicate with that person. If only we could be assured of their existence, their awareness of our thoughts and prayers for them; if only there were some way in which we could still reach them and also hear from them! The wonderful truth is that we can! In His infinite compassion, God has placed gifted mediums among us who are able to reach beyond the veil and establish a link between the realms of the living and the so-called dead.

Freddie Rivera is such an individual. A Christian Spiritualist, medium, and clairvoyant, he is able to connect with those who have passed on and communicate with them as if they were in the same room with us (and perhaps they are?). I learned about Freddie through an online group intended to provide hope and support to those who have loved ones on the other side. Over a period of several months, I observed as other members of this group provided their feedback from the mediumship readings that Freddie Rivera had done for them. Their reports were impressive, to say the least. In reading after reading, Freddie successfully connected the bereaved with loved ones who had passed on. He accurately provided names, times and circumstances of death, descriptions, and specific information that assured those left behind that their loved ones were not only fully conscious in the beyond, but were peaceful, happy, and remained fully aware of, and interested in, their ongoing earthly affairs. Again and again, I witnessed group members expressing their gratitude to Freddie Rivera for having given them evidence of their loved ones' continued existence, as well as peace of mind and heart through the opportunity of communicating with them. It was also clear to me that Freddie was a person of high integrity who was motivated by a deep desire to help others.

I have many loved ones on the other side, and I was anxious to hear from them. I decided to contact Freddie Rivera and book my own reading with him. I had had psychic readings before—some 30 years ago—but had never experienced a mediumship reading, so I didn't quite know what to expect. I was a bit nervous with anticipation as Freddie began the reading with a prayer of protection and a request to his spirit guides to allow only authentic, benevolent spirits to come through. I was hopeful, yet afraid I might be disappointed. Soon my nervousness was replaced by amazement. Each person who came through did so with very much the same personality they had had while they were still on earth, and they used "identifiers" that were authentic beyond the shadow of a doubt.

Freddie Rivera is an evidence-oriented medium; he does not want to be told anything in advance about those with whom we seek contact. Spirits are requested to come through one by one and introduce themselves with "evidence" for who they state they are. I was astounded by how quickly and accurately Freddie picked up names and the description of places and circumstances from some of my departed loved ones. In one instance there was contact with my sister, and after she identified herself, Freddie started describing the type of work that she had done. I wanted to make it easier for him and began to specify her occupation, when he assertively stated a highly specific, more accurate and more sophisticated designation of her profession, which was exactly what my sister would have done, to correct me. It was as though her personality spoke through him. Even more amazingly, my sister mentioned an upcoming celebration the following month that I was not aware of at the time of the reading. I didn't know what she meant until sometime later, when the events of that month began to unfold and my sister's comment about "a celebration in June" made perfect sense to me and my family. We were absolutely amazed at how her spirit knew about an upcoming event of which I had yet to become aware.

Another amazing fact for me was that my mother, in identifying herself, mentioned that she was with William, clearly my stepfather Bill. I had completely forgotten, but was later reminded by my husband, that my mother had always called my stepfather "William," although he was "Bill" to everyone else. You can see what I mean when I say that everyone's personality was very much unchanged from how they had been while on earth.

When my grandmother came through, she identified herself as a deeply religious woman connected with the Lutheran Church, who was offering me roses. Anyone who would have known my grandmother and the relationship I had with her would agree that this was all that was needed to establish her as my grandmother. The identifiers, though few, were so precisely on target, it was nothing short of uncanny.

Even a month later, when I think about some of the specifics that came through in the reading, I feel awe and reverence in view of what transpired. It would be impossible for the information from this reading to have been accurate by mere chance. Even telepathy, for instance if Freddie had read my mind, could not possibly account for the specifics that the reading provided. It was clear that the information came directly from my loved ones—my sister, mother, stepfather, and grandmother, who continue to exist on a plane or dimension beyond the physical world.

Freddie Rivera has an amazing gift and skill that he is employing to bring profound healing and peace to the bereaved, to those who long to know that their loved ones are still near in spirit and are eager to communicate with them. I always have been and will be among the 80 percent of the population who believe in life after death, but after my reading with Freddie, I also have direct and convincing evidence that my loved ones continue to exist in a form that I am unable to perceive with my physical senses.

Note: This is a recorded actual reading, and Clytie decided to submit it in this form. OK by me.

Clytie Koehler
San Marcos, California
http://clytiekoehler.com

Clytie is a fiction book author and Lawyer. Among her books are "Lizzy's Choice" and "Guava Gravy". She is currently working on two other books.

Mediumship Reading with Freddie Rivera, September 3, 2013

Freddie Rivera is an evidential medium. That means that he seeks evidence from Spirit to confirm that one's loved ones are communicating with him.

After explaining his work and asking to receive only positive messages and his Spirit Gatekeeper for assistance, Freddie began the reading:

There is a motherly presence coming through, a motherly presence... more like a grandmother.

She was very old, maybe in her nineties or even 100 – I have never met one so old

She was almost 103

Wow, no wonder... she had a lot of issues, things that were wrong with her – of course at that age, she would. *Yes.*

Was there congestive heart failure? *Not that I know of.* **Or something about her blood?** *I said "no" but thought about her very poor circulation at the end of her days.*

229

What was your grandmother's name? *Jessamine.* **Excuse me?** *Jessamine.* **Jessamine?** *Yes.*

She went peacefully.

She was not very tall, only about 5 'or so. *Yes, 5'2" I think but very bent over near the end*

Of course at that age she had white or grey hair. *Yes, it was white.*

She had dark eyes. *Yes, dark brown.*

I feel she was high strung, or… it is hard to place a word for her… she knew what she wanted. *Yes.*

She was well respected. There was a time when she came closer to you. *Yes, she lived with me for the last 9+ years of her life.*

She was between being and introvert and an extrovert. *I said nothing but thought: Yes, she seemed content on her own but enjoyed visiting as well.*

She is saying "July". *Yes, that is when she passed over.*

She says you have three children. *Yes*

I get something educational about her. She was a smart lady. *She was not highly educated herself, she had been to Business College but education was a high family value for her.*

She is proud of the person you have become. She loves it that you help people. She adores you. She wants to thank you for everything you did for her. *My answers to these statements were too monosyllabic to report here. I was very touched.*

Who is the lawyer? *I am.* **She loves what you went out and did for yourself.**

230

She comes around you. *I think of her often.* That is confirmation.

Is someone a Christian? I see a rosary. *No, I can't think of anyone. (But I now wonder if it was my mother's Sanyasin mala he was seeing. It is a long string of beads with a picture of Bhagwan Shri Rajneesh attached.)* Well write it down, maybe it will come to you later.

Who is Elizabeth? *I am also an author and Elizabeth is a character I write about.*

Oh, I see, you write about her? You shouldn't have told me you are an author; I might have gotten that from someone. *Oh, okay.*

There is another person around her, your grandmother, someone in Spirit. She is another mother figure. Do you have a mother in Spirit? *Yes.* She might have been in her 60s, say later than mid-sixties. *Yes. (She was 69)*

There is an "A" name, who has an "A" name who is in Spirit? *I can't think of anyone.*

Who is Alice? *Oh my gosh! Alice was my mother's best friend all of her life.*

Alice is next to her. *Oh, that's lovely!*

Your mother was 5'5" or 5'6"? *Yes or maybe even a little taller.* 5'7" then? *I think so.* 5'7" is tall for the average woman. *Yes, I suppose so.*

Do you look like your mom? You favour her in some ways? *Yes I guess so, some.*

She had blue eyes. Do you have blue eyes? *Yes, we both have blue eyes*

231

She is very apologetic. She asks you to forgive her. She wants you to forgive her for what she put you through throughout your life. Do you understand? *Yes and she doesn't need to ask for that.*

I smell smoke. There is male next to her who used to smoke a lot. Did your mom smoke?

Yes but not very much.

Your mom comes through showing that she had a lot of issues. *Yes she did.* There was something that spread throughout her body. Did she have cancer? *No, she was alcoholic and at the end it seemed that all of her organs failed. That may be where you picked up the congestive heart failure that you mentioned earlier.* Oh, that's what it was!

She says you have one sister. *Yes, that's right.*

She's still here. *Yes*

Your mom is apologetic to her as well. She wants you to give her the message. *I sure will.*

Was someone cremated? I get cremation. *Yes, both my mother and grandmother were cremated.*

She is proud of the woman that you are. *That is good to hear.*

About your being an author; I get the number 2 about your books... *Well, I have two books self-published on Amazon and I am finishing a two volume set not yet published.* Oh, yes, well that explains it.

She adores you. She comes to you in your dreams... or she has come to you in your dreams at least once. *Yes, I have dreamed of her but not a lot.* That was a visitation. That is how she makes her presence known to you.

You had a brother. *Yes*

I get a sharp pain, he crossed over. He was far away when he crossed. *Yes.*

Someone crossed him over... someone killed him! *Yes.*

He was very young... very young... maybe in his late twenties... *Yes (he was 28)*

He was doing something in another country when he crossed. *Yes.*

He was doing something... working in another country... *Yes*

He is saying "I love you too. I know how much you loved me and I love you too." *Yes, I did, thank you!*

Who is William? *That is his name!*

But they called him Bill for short, right? *Yes!*

He has good energy. He was in a bad place when he crossed. I get a Spanish speaking country. *Yes, that's right.* I meant the place he was in was bad, not the country.

What country was it? *Honduras.* Oh, Honduras.

You loved him a great deal. *Yes, I did.*

He says he had 2 children. *That's right.*

He says he knows what you have been through in life and he is proud of everything you have done. He is proud of how you have withstood it all. You are a strong woman. He loves how you went forth and made something of yourself. *I am very touched to hear that.*

Your mom yelled at me! *She did?*

Yes, your mom yelled at me. She said "1995!" *That is the year she crossed over.*

Bill, it wasn't his time to go. *It wasn't?* **No, someone crossed him over.** *Yes*

He is a protector. *Yes.* **He comes around and watches over you… like a guardian angel.**

Was he buried in a casket? *Yes. That might be where the rosary comes in because he was buried in Honduras in a Catholic ceremony because that was what they do there.* **OK.**

Your brother was not fat. *No.* **He was a skinny guy.** *He was lean, yes.*

He's showing red hair, very light – not dark red. *Yes, he had red hair, not auburn at all.*

His eyes were not dark, were they light. *They were green. My mom's and mine are blue, my grandmothers were dark brown, and Bill's were green.*

He was handsome. *Yes he was.*

About 5'9" with the same hair colour as you…

No, he was much taller than that and his hair was red.

Not as much as 6' though…

I believe he was 6'3".

Really? That tall?

Yes, I think maybe you are getting someone else. I have an idea who it might be.

234

Okay Clytie, our session is over but there is one more.

He feels familiar. He says your friend Medea; you are like a mother figure to her. You are like a mother figure to Medea. Does that make sense? *Yes!*

You are her mother! *Yes.*

It is Edwin. *Yes.* Edwin... You were divorced from him. *Yes.*

He was 5'9" and earlier in life his hair was close to the same colour as mine.

Ahh, the 5'9" I got before, feels like he was standing close to William who you said is 6' 3". He says he always loved you. *I know...*

He had lung cancer and he had to wear that thing around his throat... *Yes, I listened to Medea's reading.* You did? *Yes.*

That's good. And he was bald at the end.

He loves you; he's sorry about the way things went between you but you each had your own life paths. *I know. It was my decision to end it.*

He was a strong-willed man. *Yes*

A quiet man but he had his moments. *(Maybe quiet at the end when he couldn't talk!)*

He just came through to say hello. *Hello Ed.*

He's sending a lot of love – he wants you to give all of his children a big hug and kiss.

I will.

235

He's proud of you, too.

He wants you to keep going... the rest of your life is going to be wonderful. You are on your right path.

I am trying.

You are learning lessons.

END of READING

Physical review (key points)

I feel stress in your head, enough to throw you off.

There is something missing about your eyes... I get something missing about your eyes. *Yes*

Are you missing an eye? *Yes*

Because I only get one... *you are right.*

Do you have a lifelong battle with your weight? *Yes*

Your body flashes red. That could mean (here Freddie named off a number of possibilities, diabetes being one of them). *Yes, I am diabetic.*

You are careful what you eat, is that because of indigestion? *No, I am careful what I eat because I want to protect my health.*

Freddie then named a few minor issues and then told me he feels I am healthy.

THANK YOU FREDDIE!

236

Josie Varga
Westfield, New Jersey
http://www.josievarga.com

Josie is the author of Visits From Heaven and Divine Visits, among others.

Who is Vincenza?

Life is eternal; and love is immortal; and death is only a horizon; and a horizon is nothing save the limit of our sight. - **R.W. Raymond**

German philosopher, Arthur Schopenhauer, once said, "After your death, you will be what you were before your birth." What Schopenhauer is referring to is the fact that we are all timeless and eternal. True, the body dies so there is certainly physical death. But the soul lives on.

When we cross over, we go back to our true essence which is spirit. As Schopenhauer puts it, we will go back to being what we were before our birth. If this was not true then it would not be possible for psychic mediums such as Freddie Rivera to communicate with those on the Other Side. Afterlife communication would not be possible, or real.

Freddie contacted me after reading my book, *Visits from Heaven*, which highlights evidential afterlife communication accounts from around the world. He offered to give me a free mediumship reading and I accepted his generous offer. I believe that our loved ones on the Other Side often lead us to mediums when they want to get a message to us. For this reason, I try never to refuse a reading offer.

During the first half of the reading, I could not recognize the names Freddie gave me, but this is common if the sitter doesn't know of family members they have never met, as you will see. But when he told me that my maternal grandmother was present, he really got my attention. Since my grandmother was reportedly present, I asked him to tell her to give me a validation. This is something that I often do when I'm being given a reading. If your loved one is truly present, there is no reason why a medium would not be able to provide a validation of some sort.

I waited for a response and all of a sudden Freddie said, "Your grandmother said to tell you, Jacque." My mouth dropped and I just about fell out of my chair. Freddie had unknowingly given me a huge validation. The reading was given to me on a Thursday night. The next day I was attending the wedding of my cousin Micki's daughter, Jacque! There is no way Freddie could have known this information.

Freddie went on to tell me that my grandmother wanted me to know that she would be at the wedding in spirit. He then told me that there was someone else with my grandmother. "I'm getting the name, Vincent…no, Vincenza. Who is Vincenza?" I could not recall who Vincenza was.

"Well, she's with your grandmother so it has to be someone from your mother's side," he explained. "Write it down and ask your mother." I eagerly wrote the name down and promised to ask my mother.

The next day, as promised, I called my mother and asked her who Vincenza was. My mother didn't answer me at first and wanted to know why I was asking. "Because I had a reading with a medium last night and he told me that Nonna (grandma in Italian) was with a woman named Vincenza." I could hear my mother gasp on the other end. "Mom, who is Vincenza? I asked, again.

"Vincenza is my grandmother," my mother finally replied.

"She is your great grandmother." Obviously, this was another big validation for me. Freddie had given me information that I didn't even know. My great grandmother died before I was born and I don't remember my mother ever mentioning her name to me.

I was very close to my maternal grandmother growing up. She was always there for me and still is. Only now she is there in spirit. Like I said, spirit is our true essence and the spirit never dies. Life goes on. We go on. Love goes on. Nothing will ever break the bonds of love, not even death.

My Godmother Lucy passed away in February 2010. I was heartbroken as she was a second mother to me. Since then, I have received many signs or visits from heaven from her. I often sense when she's around and always try to acknowledge her presence.

During my reading with Freddie, my Godmother Lucy came through. Freddie told me, "She says you are very good at picking her up." Absolutely true and this was yet another validation.

My first reading with Freddie took place in July 2011; two months later I started a group on Facebook based on my book called, "Visits from Heaven." I started this group because I wanted to offer others a safe forum where they could come and share their own experiences. I wanted to help the bereaved by sharing the message that love never dies and life never ends.

Freddie joined the group and soon after offered to give free readings to the members of my Visits from Heaven Facebook group. I agreed as I felt this was a wonderful way to bring comfort to those who are grieving the loss of a loved one. Albert Einstein once said, "Only a life lived for others is a life worthwhile." I couldn't agree more and I can honestly say that Freddie Rivera is no stranger to these words.

As a result of these free readings, I received many letters from members thanking me for bringing them much sought-after comfort and helping them understand that love truly never dies. But Freddie Rivera deserves all the credit. His generosity and kind spirit do not go unnoticed. He may be a gifted psychic medium but more importantly he is also kind-hearted.

Medea Yorba
Escondido, California
https://www.facebook.com/medea.yorba

Medea is a fiction writer. Her very first book is out now
called "Darcy's Last Promise".

Elvis Is In the House

I have had plenty of readings in my life from different
mediums and also was an active medium when I was younger
(I stopped doing readings), so when I say that Freddie's gift
far surpasses any I have ever experienced, that is saying a lot.

In preparation for the reading, I had talked to and set out one
item each of the three people I really wanted to hear from.

After first explaining what and how he was going to do the
reading, we prayed of only light and benevolent spirits to
come through. He asked his *Gate Keeper*, to begin with letting
only one spirit at a time come through. He said an older
gentleman was there that had already been coming around
him before he even called me.

Then to my utter delight, he started describing my dad to a T.
He described my dad's height, little to no hair, skinny frame
and then that he was wearing a breathing apparatus around
his neck. He said that he had a hard time breathing, when he
passed. I then explained that my father had died of throat and
lung cancer. I didn't mention that my dad had his whole
inside of his throat hollowed out and could only breath
through the hole in his neck. I didn't feel I needed to explain
that part. I knew without a doubt at that point that he was
speaking with my dad.

241

While I was still in shock, I was taken by surprise by the fact that there was more jaw dropping messages to come.

My dad told Freddie that I was his daughter and that I had four kids. Freddie said that my dad was throwing names at him. He named all of my kids except for one; an MA name. He described her as the third child and that she looked just like me. The third child he spoke of is my daughter Miranda. We refer to her as my mini me. She reminded me later that my dad spelled her name Maranda. Also my youngest son has an unusual name and was the grandchild who got to spend the most time with my dad. He said, "Tell Porter I said hi and give him a hug for me". My dad had said this many times to me on the phone when he was still able to speak.

He talked of my dad's head not being clear at the end. My dad's mind was not functioning well due to the lack of oxygen to his brain. He said that my dad had worked with his hands and did maintenance. All of this was true. Then he threw me for another loop and said I get the name Ed...Ed...Edward. I got so excited I jumped up and said yes, actually forgetting for a moment my own dads name was Edwin. He spoke of my dad being determined and strong willed and having the personality that smiled and laughed a lot. He said "he adores you" many times. I was his only daughter. He also said my dad was the kind of parent who demanded respect. That comment made me laugh. My dad had disowned me for a day at a time on many occasions! Freddie also smelled cigarettes and remarked that my dad chain smoked and drank alcohol. This was also a very accurate description of my dad.

My father told Freddie that I was gifted. I felt my gift had gone away, and my dad knew that thought had left me feeling half empty. That validation from him was a nice gesture, not to mention that it gave me a sense of purpose again. He also showed Freddie my image and Freddie described me. He mentioned the military service we had for my dad's memorial. Freddie then brought up a woman with my dad. Not knowing of one on the other side except for my grandmother or aunt, I was shocked again when Freddie asked "who is Virginia?" Oh my gosh! She is my dad's girlfriend of 30 years who is very near the end of her life .We never thought my dad would go before her, as she has been sick for many years.

Freddie also acknowledged by name 'Niki'; a cousin I had raised. There were so many other messages that came out of that reading and just too many to share. My dad was so enthusiastic about getting to communicate that he took up the whole 30 minutes! It was a wonderful gift for which I will always be grateful. I was not done though, so I booked another reading for the next day. There were two other individuals that I dearly needed to hear from.

8/13/2013

My second reading,

Freddie asked me for the first name of the person I wanted to talk to. I told him David. He said he felt that the death was unnatural and asked if it had been a car accident. I acknowledged this and he said he felt something with the chest and that it was a very powerful crash (our car split in half). Freddie described David's looks and dark prominent eyes. He also saw his tattoos.

He then saw another gentleman in black. David didn't really wear black; I had a sneaking suspicion of who it was though. We just kind of let it go for the time being.

Freddie then said David wanted to convey a message "Tell Porter I love him and miss him very much." Porter is David and my son.

He felt David was unhealthy towards the end of his life. I had left David as I had no choice, and he had become very wreck – less with alcohol and prescription drugs. He had overdosed twice and was very weakened and unhealthy as a result. To add to my raw feelings of attaining word from David, he said he was very sorry for the way things had turned out. David had asked me to marry him two days before he died and I had accepted.

Freddie had felt David's torment from a very rough and painful and abusive childhood, and expressed that no matter how hard David had tried to get passed it, he just couldn't do it and he turned to alcohol and drugs.

David said I was a good mom and that things would get easier with our son when he gets older and he would be fine. Our son is autistic. He said he loved me and was sending me flowers. Freddie said they were all different kinds of flowers, that I didn't have a favorite. He said he saw wild flowers. I laughed; David used to tease me because I picked bouquets of wild flowers and even added weeds if they were pretty. The reading with David was wonderful and full of many more messages.

Again one of my loved ones took up almost the whole reading. So we decided to quickly do one more because I wanted to hear from this other person and said it would be very short. I only needed validation that he was still with me; I hadn't felt him lately and we had made a deal years ago.

Freddie asked me for his first name. I paused and explained that this person had been with me since I was twelve, just after his death and that I couldn't say his name because he was famous. Freddie then said "Is it Elvis Presley? Elvis is here." That's all I needed. Elvis first appeared to me when I was twelve and had always stuck with me. He also came through on three other occasions with three other mediums. We have shared past lives as cousins. Our deal is that he is going to be the one who helps me transition and cross over when it is time. He acknowledged to Freddie that he still would. Before we hung up the phone, we knew who the man in black was. I really thought it was funny when I realized that I had an Elvis mug not three feet in front of me and he was dressed in black!

I will always be so grateful for these very special readings and look forward to more readings with Freddie in the Future. The message from my dad about still being gifted has also left me a little inspired to revisit that part of my life again. Maybe I just needed a break.

Again thank you so much Freddie, for the visit with my loved ones.

Medea Yorba

Kathleen Theresa Ferber Eggert
Levittown, Pennsylvania
https://www.facebook.com/kathleen.f.eggert

Kathleen is a Minister, Teacher and Counselor.

The Flowers

When I lost both of my parents; they were some of the hardest years of my life. I had been in a very deep, dark, depression for a number of years, and my quality of life had plummeted further and further. I had finally decided enough is enough when my wonderful son said it was time to stop grieving, and start concentrating on those who were still living, and who loved me.

At that point I took a few classes at the community college in Spirituality; Past Lives Theory, Intuitiveness and Creativeness.

After one of these classes and an e-mail from one of the professors, I had been put in contact with a woman by the name of Christine Dominiak. She had a radio show. Christine sent me an e-mail about a woman who was writing a book based on contact from loved ones on to the afterlife. She asked me to share some of my visits or signs with the author.

After the author read my story, she said she was "Guided" to sign me on with her group. She also said that I would meet people that "will listen and stand by you, and who are likeminded." I had no idea at the time that this wonderful compassionate group of people would change my life for the better forever!

I had a card reading once with a woman who claimed to be

246

intuitive. I didn't take a great deal away from the experience, because everything she told me was much too vague. I felt like it was a blanket reading, and that she was giving only the meaning of the cards; there was no intuition involved or being used.

I absolutely know that we can communicate with those who have physically died, most definitely. I've had many signs from my loved ones; I can feel their warm hands on my back at times. There are a total of six that were close to me that have passed.

My father spoke to me through a television show that had a medium; he gave me a sign of snow falling only over our house on the 1st Christmas after he had passed. My mother and daughter were both present to see this.

My mother left beautiful small pink flowers all over my car three weeks after her passing; in the middle of winter one morning. No flowers were found anywhere else on my property. The car parked right next to it in the driveway had nothing. There were none on the ground or trees. They were only on my car.

Amazingly, at a later time when I had a reading with Freddie, he told me that my mother communicates with me sometimes with flowers.

The same morning I had found the flowers, I found a birthday card from her that had a sticker sealing the envelope with a flower identical to the ones on my car. The card had a prayer on it; "You can get through anything."

When my husband's Uncle Bobbie had passed, (we had been friends on Facebook and we used to banter and kid a lot). My cover photo would change to his picture all by itself. It had also changed to pictures of flowers the day I planted a garden in his honor.

My niece passed away at the age of twenty-four a few years ago at the hands of a doctor, who misdiagnosed her case. My husband and I were discussing the possibility of her parents suing the hospital and the doctor. At that moment during the discussion, the lights in my kitchen went on by themselves.

On the morning of the day Freddie was to call to give me the reading, my husband and I were leaving work. We got to the door and opened it. A breeze blew by, and the scent of fresh beautiful roses passed by us. I knew it was my mother.

I know that there is life after death, just as well as I know my name. I needed closure for my daughter who had a nervous breakdown the year my mother had passed away. She had been very close to both of my parents, and she just couldn't handle their deaths. She spent months crying, and I needed the healing process to begin for her before it was too late. I needed validation that all of my experiences were real; that I wasn't dreaming these beautiful signs up in my head. I needed to know that my loved ones who had passed were at peace, not in pain. I needed to know that they are with God and happy and that my mom and dad were together again. I also needed to know that those warm hands on my back were exactly what I had felt they were.

Freddie called, and my daughter was allowed to sit in during the reading. I have to admit I was a little taken back at first when he began speaking of a "Gatekeeper" and how the reading began since I'd never experienced anything like this.

As I began to settle in, a man with the letter J stepped forward. "Jo sounding like John", Freddie said. It was my uncle Johnnie. How appropriate that he came forward at the very beginning as he had been the first person in my life to pass away. I was sixteen at the time and was very upset. He'd lived right next door and just before he had become ill, he'd come to visit with us every night around dinner time. My uncle was a sweet man who whistled while he walked from their house to ours, and sang while we ate dinner. I had missed him terribly when he stopped coming. A few months after, he was diagnosed with lung cancer and passed away within that year.

During the reading Freddie told me he said he was sorry for hurting me, for staying away. Freddie also described him; there was no mistake that it was my uncle Johnnie.

Freddie then brought forward a man with blue eyes and light colored hair. The letter "A; Albert" he said. It was my dad (Chick by nickname). He said that he loved me, was proud of the woman I had become, and proud of the mother I was. He said that he knew I was now a grandmother, and that they had seen the babies before they were born. He told me my parents had lived in a light-colored house by water. The house was around the corner from a huge lake. He said that my dad was happy and was with his two dogs, and that he had a boat. Freddie saw my dad and the dogs on the lake in the boat. My father always wanted a boat. He said he felt no more pain, and that he knew my dad was unable to speak for some time before his death.

He also validated that my Dad knew I was with him when he passed, and that he knew my children were there as well.

Freddie told me my mom was with him, that they were together again. That my mom's name started with an "M" "Mary", he said accurately. She had salt and pepper hair and was quiet, not much to say, but she knew we were having the reading that night and the scent of roses we had smelled was from her telling us; she knew of the reading.

Freddie knew of the pain in her head that had caused her death. She had a brain aneurysm. He knew I spent one night alone with her in her hospital room quietly speaking to her; I had massaged her arms and legs, touched her face and head, and I told her it was ok to let go. He told me the signs I had been receiving were from them and that the hands on my back were from all of those loved ones that had passed "Had my back." This confirmed to me the six hands I felt were theirs.

Freddie has done more than one reading on me. The second was to be of guidance to my life's path. We discussed how my spiritual journey had just begun, and I was to join a group of like-minded individuals who I would be able to feel comfortable with and grow spiritually. He also began speaking of my two brothers telling me that one of them had heart problems. Within three days, one of my brothers was admitted into the hospital with an irregular heartbeat.

He had also told me that this brother would be hurting me in the near future. I couldn't even imagine that, but it was true. Within eight months, he had decided to walk out of my life since he didn't like me becoming this new "Spiritual" person.

Freddie also shared that my other brother and I had issues; I didn't want to mention them here, but Freddie was right on about them.

Freddie took it upon himself when I became very ill two years ago January to call me at home on a Saturday evening and spend almost two hours with me. He did a long-distance Reiki healing on me, and taught me how to cleanse and align my chakra's. He taught me how to say a protective prayer, how to ground and center myself. I slept for an entire night for the first time that very night. That was a miracle at that time in itself!

After going over everything that had transpired that evening and the next few days, and reading the notes I had written, things became much clearer. A million-pound weight was lifted. The grieving process began to dissipate right then and there.

The entire next year was spent healing and learning, and Freddie, has been there for me every step of the way. He is my "Spiritual Mentor." He has changed my life for the better; he has completely helped in my healing process and is playing a huge part in my life; entirely turning 180 degrees in a different direction.

Since he has been guiding me, I have earned my Bachelor's Degree in Philosophy/Metaphysical Sciences and have taken my vows to become a Minister/Teacher/Counselor. I am currently a student of Thanatology hoping to do work in grief counseling for children and also work in hospice in some capacity. I volunteer at an assisted-living facility and will be volunteering to work at a facility to counsel children who have lost loved ones.

I am finally at peace in my life now, happier than I've ever been and owe a great deal of it to this wonderful caring person. These readings have given me the closure that was needed for me to move forward with my life, and to find peace and happiness within myself; to find a new passion and possibly a brighter future. I now have everything I need to be whole again. I love this man, my dear friend Freddie Rivera!

Billie Layland
Clarendon, Texas
https://www.facebook.com/billie.molder

Shirt off His Back

I was a bit nervous when Freddie called me to give me my reading. My son Michael came through. He told me that Michael's death was an unnatural one. He crossed himself over.

Michael committed suicide by hanging in April of 2006. At first, Michael was hesitant to come forward, but Freddie felt his presence and asked him to communicate. He said he was sorry for what he put me through, but he wanted me to move forward with my life, and that it would make him happy if I did. I miss him with all my heart and still have tears that won't stop, but I feel as close to him now as I did before he passed. He is doing alright.

Michael was the kind of person that would give you the shirt off his back. The following really hit home because of its accuracy.

Freddie told me that he was mentioning a female cousin of his by the name of Micki. Michael was staying with Micki, and later I found out that she helped him learn to tie a noose, but she didn't know what his intentions were. He committed suicide in her home. There were many things that Freddie mentioned that I could validate as truth.

Sarah Kovalsky came through. She was my friend; we met on an online therapy group. At the time, I didn't know that she was dying of cirrhosis of the liver. Sarah lost her son on

252

March 4th of 2007, also to a suicide. Freddie described her exactly, and told me of what she died from. She had some very special messages for me. I was grateful that she came through. She gave Freddie the number five, telling me that she passed away five days after Michael did.

My mother-in-law, Ruthann Layland, was the last one to come through. My husband Ray and I made a trip to West Palm Beach Florida on Thanksgiving. It was a year before we married. That was the first time I ever saw Ruthann. She was living in an assisted living center there. Freddie felt a mother's presence. He said she has a double name. Then he said Ann. He mentioned that there was another part to her name that began with an R letter. He also told me that she was in her mid-eighties when she passed; she was 85.

Ruthann and her first daughter in law, didn't get along well. I could tell she felt the same way about me. Her husband had passed a couple of years before from liver cancer, and she was in a deep depression. Maybe she would have felt better if we hadn't married, but we didn't feel we could do things for someone else; even his mother.

While in Florida, her daughter Linda was caring for her. Sometime after our visit, the assisted care facility decided she needed total care. Linda was leaving to travel for her job.

By that time we were married, we asked her to come to the care – facility; here where we live. She wasn't happy because the facility here was nothing compared to what her money could buy her in West Palm Beach.

My husband Ray made daily trips to see her, but we waited a bit to give her time to adjust to the new facility. One morning, as Ray was getting ready to visit his mom, the care center called to tell us that she had just passed. That was the week after she got here. I know she must be happier now than when she was here physically alive. I will never know why she really didn't care for me, except that I didn't come from money; our lifestyles were terribly different. During the reading she assured me that she has now accepted me and was apologetic for the way she treated me. Having her give that message from the other side, gave me a sense of peace on which I hadn't counted on.

Freddie had told me that Ruthann died peacefully in her sleep; he was correct.

I have no doubt that we can communicate with those who have crossed over. I know that the spirit world is here on earth, but the majority of us aren't able to pick up on them the way mediums do. I can ask my son for a hug, wrap my arms around myself and feel his energy Corse through my veins. He was always big on hugs for mom. Looking back he spent about four of his last five months with me, and every time he passed me, he asked for a hug.

I actually needed a visit from heaven and God, and my son knew that. I am a woman of great faith and truly believe that if I pray for something, God will answer my prayers and provide a way to comfort me. I thank you Freddie, for the reading that gave me such comfort.

I had to have a mediumship reading or die to be with my son. My loss was more than I could bear, and I wasn't dealing well with is death. I still have days that are more than I can deal with; although I knew if I could just make contact with my precious boy, that I would remain here on God's earth and follow his plan for me. Now I can wait until I am called back home with God. I know that I will again see my son and my other dear family members that are waiting there for me.

Because Mike was hesitant to come forward at first, and required some encouragement, I was afraid that I would miss out on him. During the reading, I can remember Michael trying to explain how he took his life and how he was sorry because he never wanted to hurt me. Freddie told me after the reading, that Michael was ashamed. That is the reason he was hesitant; then started to open up. I am so glad that he did.

I continue to worry, but that is the human part of me. The spiritual part, tells me that he is beyond temptation and mental illness. He is with God, and nothing will hurt him again.

Michael would have been diagnosed with Attention deficit-hyperactivity disorder (ADHD) if there had been a diagnosis of that when he was young. There was no day that he wasn't in trouble about something, and he was raised with an abusive father figure. He always wanted a friend but never found one. He was my oldest, and the younger kids had their little groups. Anytime he would come in the house, looking for adult attention, he was told by the father figure to go away and find something to do.

Michael was always misunderstood and taken for granted. The only person he truly knew loved him was me; his mom. The reading has made me feel a whole lot better. It is always said that those that take their own lives don't go to Heaven, but that is far from the truth. My son is in Heaven.

Kalila Smith
New Orleans, Louisiana
http://www.kalilasmith.com

Kalila was born and raised in New Orleans. She personally researched and wrote the material featured on Haunted History Tours of New Orleans' Ghost, Vampire and Voodoo tours. She is the author of New Orleans Ghosts, Voodoo, & Vampires, Tales From the French Quarter, Farewell, My Forever Child, and Miami's Dark Tales. Her newest book is Afterlife Mysteries Revealed.

I Want Pizza Too

After my daughter's sudden death in January, 2013, I consulted several mediums to connect with her for messages. One of them was Freddie Rivera. Freddie conducted his sessions by phone. I was very curious about this method of mediumship as the sitter was not in front of the medium; so no face to face contact. This would seem to be more difficult but not for Freddie.

Like most mediums he began his session explaining how it worked for him. Once he had done that, he asked his "gate keeper" to allow the first contact to speak to him. He described a man that could be no one other than my father who had died when I was eighteen years old; thirty-seven years earlier!

Freddie described my father to a tee. He immediately tuned into the estranged relationship that I had shared with him. He told me that my father was sorry for the distance that he had put between us during his life. He also expressed that he was proud of me and encouraged me to write more. Freddie then said that my father was with two other people. He said the woman had an "M" name like "Margaret." He also said the number four.

My father had four siblings, one of whom was his sister Margaret. He then asked me if I knew someone named "Robert."

My Aunt Margaret was married to my Uncle Bob. This was definitely my father that was coming through and this was my validation. Freddie then said there was someone with a name that began with "L." At the time, this made no sense to me other than that my maiden name began with "L." Later that evening, I remembered that my father's other sister was my Aunt Lily. My father's visit was just the beginning in what was to turn out as an incredible reading. There was much more to come.

My mother then stepped forward and again, Freddie described her in the finest details. I was pleased to learn that my parents were still very much a couple and soul mates on the other side. They had been together since they were very young and spent their entire lives together. I had read in many sources that married couples continue as couples together in the afterlife, this seemed to validate that school of thought. I don't know what that means for the rest of us. I should have asked because I cannot help but wonder if those of us who are alone in this life, without a significant other, continue the same in the afterlife.

Freddie told me that my mother spoke of someone named "Kathy" and he was confused as to whether it was a "C" or a "K" name. I was absolutely blown away by this! My mother's name was Carrie. My birth name was Kathy. I legally changed my name to Kalila after using the name as a stage name during my many years as a performance artist, then as a pen name as an author.

My parents mentioned the month of March. This could only connect to my deceased daughter whose birthday is March 1. Stephanie died from an obscure infection following what should have been a routine outpatient surgical procedure. Freddie immediately tuned into Stephanie's child-like nature and asked me if she was "special." I told him that he was correct. Stephanie had Down Syndrome. Although she was almost thirty when she died, her energy was more like a younger child.

Freddie amazed me when he delivered what he felt was a strange message from Stephanie. He hesitated and said, "She said, 'Hey I like pizza too, bring me a piece.' I don't know why she is talking about pizza."

I couldn't believe he told me that! Unbeknownst to Freddie, I was in my car on my mobile phone sitting outside a pizza restaurant, waiting for my granddaughter to pick up an order. There was absolutely no way that he could have possibly known that. Stephanie, no doubt, knew where I was! Also, he said it exactly the way she would have. This was not a coincidence, he had communicated with her.

Freddie had no way of knowing what I had done earlier that day. This was All Souls Day. It is the day in the Catholic Church as well as in other traditions such as Santeria. We honor the souls who have passed and continue their spiritual lessons in hopes of ascending to their highest potential. I had spent the morning with my godparents cleaning the graves of several people who were buried in Holt Cemetery; a city cemetery for those who cannot afford private cemeteries. I had chosen to clean the grave of an unnamed baby boy who died in 2011.

In addition to honoring this unknown child and others who were buried there, I remembered my own unnamed child that was lost to miscarriage in 1981. That baby would have been my middle child. In the 1980s, babies who died that early were unceremoniously disposed of by the hospital, and bereaved mothers were given no sympathy for their loss. It was assumed that the mother was "young and able to have another child." Although I grieved deeply for this child, I was very young and hardly grieved properly for the loss. I did the socially accepted thing at the time and pushed my grief inside. I remained heartbroken over the loss until Stephanie's birth, when I was able to move forward past the pain. Although it was too early to determine the sex of the baby, I had always imagined that is was a boy. I had picked out the name Christopher, but not a girl's name, even though it might have been a girl for all I knew. I shared the story with my godparents and we called the baby in the unmarked grave, Christopher Doe.

I then told my godparents that I often wondered if Stephanie met her unborn sibling on the other side. Later that evening, when I spoke to Freddie, that question was answered. After Freddie delivered the message about the pizza he told me that Stephanie said that she did not have a brother but a sister on the other side. He asked if I had miscarried. I was again blown away by this information. I made a comment that I had been calling the baby Christopher but all the while it was a Christina.

On the night of my reading, Stephanie appeared to me in a dream and informed me that her sister's name is Jennifer. When my oldest daughter was a young child, she always wanted a baby sister and wanted to name her Jennifer. When I had Stephanie, my oldest even called her Jennifer when she was first born. It took a while for her to grow accustomed to calling her Stephanie. All throughout Stephanie's life, she always said she had two sisters. I would always correct her and say, "You have only one sister."

She would always respond, "No, I have two."

This would explain why the butterflies always appear in pairs. There are always two butterflies that show up together, one from Stephanie and the other from the daughter that I never got to know. The one message that she did give to me in the dream was that she is where she came from. She said, "This is where we all come from; I am home."

This revelation also validated a previous reading I had in June from an artist medium who said that Stephanie kept telling her a name that started with a "J." This medium even said the name "Jen."

It is common that mediums will see, hear or feel something that the sitter does not readily recognize. During my reading with Freddie, he kept asking me about someone whose name started with an "A." He said "Annie" or "Anna." He also said she would have been a grandmother or grandmother figure. All of my grandparents were deceased by the time I was born so I did not know any of them. I did however know that no one went by that name. So this name, like "Jen" in June, made no sense to me at the time. I later learned from a cousin that my Aunt Lily's first name was Anna.

I was amazed by Freddie's medium reading and I later used him again for a psychic reading. I and was equally impressed. Thank you, Freddie!

Angie Pechak Printup
Southaven, Mississippi
HeBlewHerAKiss.com

Angie is the co-author/co-editor of two books on true After Death Communication Stories, affirming that life and love are eternal, called "He Blew Her a Kiss."

J...Jo...John

Most of us experience difficulties in life, but one of the hardest to overcome is the loss of a loved one. Simple things we took for granted such as conversations and touch are suddenly ripped away from us, creating a void and overwhelming sense of loneliness. Everyone handles their grief journey differently and there is no "one way" to travel down this path. Fortunately, there are many tools to help us on our day-to-day walk.

Although I am involved in after death communication (ADC) work and truly believe we are spiritual beings having a human experience, I, like most, experience the same emotions and grief from losing a loved one. However, by embracing what I have learned of after-death communication and truly believing that our loved ones live on, I have found great peace in knowing we are able to receive signs from our loved ones (ADCs) and that it is even possible to communicate with them through a medium.

A gifted medium can bridge the gap between the two worlds allowing our loved ones to communicate they are still with us and part of our day-to-day life. One such gifted medium is Freddie Rivera. I found Freddie on a Facebook page. I read numerous comments on readings he gave people validating their loved ones existence on the other side. I decided to contact him for I wanted so much to connect with my Dad.

I lost my Dad in 2005, and we were extremely close. I am the youngest of 5 children, the 4 oldest being boys. Dad and I were tight! I have often asked him for a sign and thought I was being open, but never really felt his presence. When Freddie called me for my reading I found out almost instantly how extremely gifted he is. He also has a very kind and gentle spirit. You immediately pick up on his "authenticity" after the first minute he begins speaking with you. Beforehand, he doesn't want to know anything about you. The only thing he asks is for you to send him a picture of yourself ahead of time.

After a brief prayer he began to communicate with the spirits asking them to come through one at a time. Immediately my grandmother on my Dad's side came through and he named her by her first name, Mary. I didn't know her for she died when my Dad was fourteen.

After a few minutes he thanked her and asked for the next spirit to come through. He began describing a man whom he said was very close to me, whose first name was J – Jo – John. He told me this was my father. I was amazed. That was my Dad's first name. Not only did he describe him physically to a T, he also nailed my dad's incredible personality. He described my dad's occupation and every piece of information he gave me was accurate. I was so excited and truly felt he was indeed communicating with my dad.

He then began naming off other relatives who were with my Dad, and also a friend. He named my uncle Bob (Dad's brother whom he often called Robert). Freddie then asked me "who was the nurse?" That was my aunt who was married to my Uncle Bob. He also said a big brown dog was by Dad's side and was his favorite. I knew exactly who that was – our Akita, Suki. We had many Akitas growing up but Suki was the family favorite. Freddie even described the color of my Dad's house and a nearby lake that he enjoyed walking around.

There were a few others who came through who I did not recognize, but these may have been people in my Dad's life that I did not know.

Freddie then hit me with something I didn't see coming. He asked if I had lost any children because he was seeing two children with my dad. My initial response was no because I have no children. Then my thoughts raced back to many years ago. I did experience two early pregnancies that ended in miscarriages at about 7 weeks. Losing them in such an early stage of the pregnancy I never knew what sex they were. Freddie said Dad had my two children with him and they were a boy and a girl. Although I was so overcome with emotions at this point, it brought much peace and comfort to me. Dad told Freddie to tell me they would be waiting for me. What an amazing reunion to look forward to.

The last question Freddie wanted me to clarify was who was doing the work in grief, bereavement and after death communication. I said it was me. He told me my Dad was very aware of this and proud of me and to keep up the good work. There is no way Freddie could have realized how significant that message was for me. My dad was a devout Catholic his entire life and I always wondered what he thought of the path I was now following. Now with Freddie's assistance I had my answer. Hearing my dad's message only confirmed what I believe with all my heart. Our loved ones do live on and they can and will communicate with us through various means.

All of what Freddie conveyed to me was validation that it was indeed my Dad coming through. As we were coming to the end of the reading Freddie asked my Dad for a message for me. Dad said that he loved me very much, was very proud of me and that he comes around a lot to see me and that I just need to be more open to his presence. I had to laugh because I thought I "was" being open, doing the work that I do. I can assure you I am even more open now!

Trina Trimm King
Oklahoma City, Oklahoma
https://www.facebook.com/trina.t.king
Foundation: http://www.mafiafoundation.org

Hey Mom Quit Smoking!

I had my reading with Freddie on a Sunday night. I was *not disappointed* at all! In fact, I tried to prepare myself mentally and even went as far as investing in a digital recorder so that I could tape the conversation with his permission; I would be able to play back the reading in case I missed something or couldn't remember what he said. I do have brain fog due to my deep grief. I also took notes to go back over if there was something I needed to clarify or revalidate.

Freddie, *you my friend*, are the authentic real deal. You have been blessed with this beautiful gift to share with others.

First let me say "Thank You!" You have helped me more than you could possibly know and there are simply no words that can articulate what your reading meant and means to me. I am grateful that you helped me!

Freddie as you know, I was a little nervous at first, but you made me feel at ease pretty much right away. What you don't know is that before you called me, and you were right on the dot with the time, is that I surrounded myself with pictures of my loved ones, and belongings of them and white candles. And yes, I drank plenty of water!

Freddie explained how he works and we moved forward with his reading. He first brought through my maternal grandfather. His picture was one that I mentioned. At the

265

beginning, I wasn't sure. I thought it might be someone else close to me, but it was evident that it was my grandfather. I never had the honor of his memory because he passed away when I was 10 or 11 months old. Freddie gave me his name and his middle name and also was able to tell me how he passed and what his health issues were. My grandfather passed away with a massive heart attack. In fact, when he had it, I was sitting on his lap. Everything he told me about my grandfather was in line with everything I was ever told about him.

Yes Freddie, he was a hardworking man that commanded respect, but was kind and loved his family. He picked cotton during the Depression and then worked at a glass plant with one lung to boot. It was great to hear from him as I always heard so many stories about him and never had the privilege of knowing him. He passed at 70 years old; looking at my records.

Then Freddie brought through Mary, my Mom. She was with her father, John Robert; my grandfather. My mother passed in 2006 and that was the most grief stricken and devastated I had ever been, with the loss of her. I don't even remember the first year after her passing. She was my rock, my best friend and we did everything together. She helped me raise my kids and was in their lives every day. Freddie was able to validate through many things that it was her; from where she worked, in the VA Hospital, to our next door neighbor and friend, Joanne. We lived side by side with Joanne for many years and my mom and her were very good friends. He brought through her personality as well. And yes Freddie, she was a very outspoken woman (extravert) and if you didn't want her opinion, you better not ask; sometimes you might have gotten it anyway.

LOL (Laughing Out Loud). She was beautiful inside and out

266

and loved by many. She was a neat lady and I have been told by some that she was "Hollywood Beautiful." I am grateful that God blessed me with her as my mother. I have always said that if I could be half the woman she was, I would be doing ok. You told me she had two siblings, and that is correct. You also detected her heart troubles and breast cancer. She was a seven year Breast Cancer Survivor, and when it came back, it came back fast and furious. You said that you felt it all through her body. And yes, it spread to her bones. You mentioned her head. I am thinking that when I brought her home from the hospital and brought hospice in, that maybe it was because she was so medicated for pain. I don't know that for sure, but my gut tells me so. In the days before her passing, with chemo and her meds, she was in and out with lucidity. I watched her carry on conversations with her lost loved ones and listened.

I knew she was tired and was done with chemo. We agreed to stop and take her home. I only had her home for a few days before she passed. Our hospice team was amazing and I know their job is to make the person as comfortable as possible. My mom was aware and lucid when I got her home and was talking and happy to be home. And when hospice came in, they made sure she wasn't in pain, but unfortunately, that meant that she was sleeping and not conscious much. The night before she passed, I knew that the time was close. I didn't want her to be in pain, but I also wanted her to be able to communicate if she could. So I cut back a little bit on her meds and knew that if she was in distress or pain, I could give her more.

I feel like I made the right decision there. She was able to call for me and speak her last beautiful words to me. I was with my Mom when she passed. I have always felt that was both a blessing and a curse. Freddie, *I know* she saw Angels and loved ones in the room. I could feel them too! And Oh My

Gosh! To know that our cat, Perseus was with my Mom, was so awesome! We loved that cat! He was a 25 lb. orange and white long haired tabby. Heart smiles! You also smelled smoke. My mother smoked. And I believe my grandfather smoked pipes too. I am going to double verify that tomorrow.

Ok, before I get to the hardest part for me, let me mention a couple of other things. You brought through a "William" or "Bill". I identified him as my husband's maternal grandfather. You also mentioned a "Joseph". Well, today I clarified that. My husband's grandfather's name is William Joseph Thompson. He was called Bill. He passed in 1997 and lived in PA. I have never met him, nor had my children. It was good to know that he wanted to say hi and that he was there with other loved ones. You asked me if February meant anything to me. Well that was his birth month. That is also my husbands; his grandson. Bill's birthday is the 23rd of Feb and my husbands is the 21st of Feb.

Freddie, you mentioned that you felt that there were a lot of spirits in line that wanted to communicate. You said that they were busy or pushy or something along those lines, LOL. With that being said, I am sure I will be in touch to do a full reading with you later.

Now for the hardest part for me, Freddie; you said that Mary had a young male with her. You described him to me as a blonde or dirty blonde haired young male. You said he had blue eyes. You said he didn't identify his name and you didn't know why, but that you felt a deep connection with us and with my loved ones that had already come through in the reading. That there were family lines there. That he was a teenager and that he passed from an accident. You said that for whatever reason, it was his karmic destiny to have a short life here on earth. That he comes to visit often and messes with my electronics and lights and even hangs out with our dog Sadie.

I validated you that I have seen our dog and cats behave oddly and follow things with their eyes that I can't see. They sometimes appear to chase air either with just their eyes or even their little bodies. I have had so many things happen, that at first I thought I was done gone on the crazy bus. I can't articulate it, but I have felt chills or goose bumps and the hair will stand on my arms. As though, I am being lightly touched. I have had coins appear, when I know that they were not there before. Music has changed on its own in the car. I have seen white glimmers out of my peripheral vision. My laptop times out, and the screen should stay blacked out. It will come back on all by itself. Lights flicker and I see dragonflies, butterflies, hummingbirds and even grasshoppers. There are so many things that happen. The smell of his cologne, or just that dirty little boy smell (Mom's know what I speak of; puppy dog smells and snails LOL). I have pictures with pink orbs and other colors. Too much to say but you get my drift.

He showed you a notebook or tablet and you wondered if he was an artist or liked to draw. The composition notebook that I had next to me while you were doing my reading was one of his. I was writing notes in it. In that notebook is a few of his drawings. You said "He knows how much I love him and that he loves me. That we will see each other again; that he will come to me in my dreams; *A vivid one*." I have dreamed of him, but in the sense that I am waiting for him. That I know he is there and I can feel him but he is out of sight. I am banking on that Freddie. Big time! Praying that it is so!

My youngest son, Trey, is my lil snuggle bunny and music man. He was a Momma's boy and didn't care who knew it.

He embraced life with such exuberance and was a total boy. He was handsome, not just because I am his Mom and am partial. LOL. Freddie you laughed when you said "He wore cologne at 13?" Yes, he was a lil ladies' man and the girls loved him. He played hard and loved hard. He was an awesome athlete and friend to many, and a loving son. I also want to say that before I shared your message with my husband, Trey's Dad, he told me that he had a vivid dream of Trey last night. He said he thought it really happened. He saw him in his dream and grabbed him and hugged him and he was wearing a bright yellow shirt.

Trey didn't say anything to him but he was so overwhelmed with the dream, that he woke up with a jerk and can't shake it. I told him that it sounded as if he had a dream visitation. I could go on and on. But I feel like I have been silent for so long, I wanted to get my point across. Guess I am ready to talk. Freddie you simply Rock! I know there is no way possible you would be able to know the things you shared with me. You validated so many things and I am forever grateful for the help in healing that you have given me.

Today, 9/25/12, is 10 months since I lost my Trey. I don't know what tomorrow holds, but knowing that he is okay, and my other loved ones are okay and are together, brings me so much comfort; they are still with me, just in spirit form and that we will eventually see each other again. I love the signs. They do bring me comfort when I am at my lowest. The hardest part for me was Trey saying that "I want you to move on and that he is ok and that we will see each other again."

Thank you again and God Bless You Freddie.

Much Love,

Trina King

Sep 13, 2013

I wanted to share how my most recent reading with Freddie Rivera went. This is not the first time I have had a reading with Freddie. He read for me the first time on Sep 23, 2012. He was very accurate in that reading and validated and gave me much needed healing on the loss of my youngest son, Trey. Today is 22 months since he left for Heaven. I posted in a Facebook group on Aug 5, asking for prayers on the eve of launching a foundation in memory of my son; telling his story for the first time publicly. At that time, I was hoping that Freddie would be able to read for me again. I wanted one before the story aired; with that in mind, I didn't post anything that I knew could compromise our reading. Any information he could give me, could not be found anywhere else, or was already made public. With that being said, he was aware of my post. The heart of the matter, nobody else could know. Yet again, Freddie blew me away with his accuracy, and brought much needed validations and healing.

Freddie first brought through my son, Trey. He said that he could see him in his mind's eye and Trey said, "Hey Mom!" That was pretty much how he always addressed me when he was trying to get my attention. He talked *all the time*. LOL "Hey Mom" was like every 5 minutes with questions and wanting to talk. I could actually hear him in my own head, when Freddie told me that. He also said that he had a huge smile for me.

So now, I am going to tell on myself by sharing the next part. He said that Trey said I hadn't quit smoking yet. This came up in our first reading and he said Trey really wanted me to quit smoking. Well I have to be brutally honest here. Since losing Trey, I have smoked more than ever! I know I need to quit and I am going to. I recently purchased an electronic cigarette and I am hoping that will give me the edge I need to put it down, as I have tried in the past and have picked them back up several times. I may even do hypnosis; I can't take the Zyban or the medicine with anti-depressants in them.

Moving forward a little bit, Freddie said that he was picking up on a "J" name or a "J L" name. Well before I go any further, I need to tell you that in my first reading with Freddie, he brought through my maternal grandfather whose name is John. At that time, he was saying he was getting a "J" name and I thought at first it was my father who passed six months before my son did. It turned out to be my grandfather whom I was so grateful and appreciative to get a message from. I never knew him; he passed when I was like ten months old. But at the same time, I was upset that my Dad didn't come through. I have fretted over that for a year now. Why didn't my Dad come through at my first reading with Freddie? Especially, since he passed six months before my son.

As we continued, I was able to determine that it was definitely my Dad that he was seeing and talking to. He revealed how he perceived my dad's demeanor, personality, etc. He said that he was feeling something with his chest, and my dad passed away from a massive heart attack. He mentioned that he felt something that spread through his body. My Dad had arthritis that he struggled with for many years prior to his passing. Freddie told me that he believes I favor him. I have been told that many times. He said that he wanted to acknowledge an "M" name that was associated with him and that he loves. I asked Freddie if she was in spirit or still here in the physical world, and he said he felt she was still here. That would be my Dads wife, my stepmother, and her name is Myrna.

272

He said that he was feeling the number three. My dad is one of three siblings. He also has three children. He said that he could smell tobacco, and that would be affirmative as my dad smoked cigarettes in his earlier years. He switched to smoking cigars and pipe tobacco. I remember the aroma of his tobacco pipe smelling of vanilla. He said that my dad liked to get his hands dirty and worked with his hands. This is true; his career was with heavy equipment, and he also built a private airplane in our garage when I was little. He worked on highways, served time in the military, drove tractors and operated and maintained logging equipment. He retired as a manager supervisor for Weyerhaeuser in Malaysia. He validated that my Dad had his own personal trucks and that he lived by lots of land and by water. He also validated that he was a dog lover and this I know to be true. He said that he was a strict man who liked respect and was in between an introvert and an extrovert; If he knew you, he would be more open and social and talkative. If not, then not so much.

All was true from what I remember and know of my dad. He told Freddie to reassure me that Trey was okay and was with him and a lot of family on the other side; not to worry and that Trey was not alone. He also said that my dad and Trey were playing football together and that they were making time to have some fun.

Trey had started playing football a few years before he passed and he loved it. One of the last pictures I have of Trey is in his football jersey for his school pictures. He is my little #37 and I treasure those pictures and memories of him on the football field.

Freddie said that there was a Tom with them as well, and that Trey was standing in between the two of them. Thomas is my dad's father and he passed before I was born. He was coming forward to say hello and acknowledge me and say "I'm your Grandfather". Tom's message was also please not to worry about Trey. "He is with family and we will all see each other again. They know it is hard for me and that they want me to move forward; be happy and to know Trey is where we all come from and with family."

Freddie also told me that he felt animosity or anger somehow in my relationship with my dad. Okay, this is where I think that sometimes even though you may think you need to hear one thing or something in particular; spirit knows what you really need to hear at certain times in your life or journey. There was a lot of distance between myself and my Dad and those feelings have haunted me for years. When he passed away, I flew to the Philippines to lay him to rest. He had lived across the world from me since the time I was three years of age. Without going further into more details, suffice it to say, that it was hard and I have struggled with it for my entire life. Freddie said that my Dad was asking for my forgiveness and that he wanted to apologize. That he wished we would or could have been closer. I really needed to hear that more than anyone could ever truly know. It has helped bring some healing and closure to some insecurities and unrests within myself; in regards to my dad not being present in my life and choosing to stay in that part of the world.

Freddie said that he felt that I was having and facing some tough lessons in this lifetime, that I was being tested. I have many things that I am trying to work through in my personal life, besides that of this terrible grief stricken journey of losing my son. These challenges are testing my mettle and in doing so, I am trying to deal with them with integrity and character. I am trying to let go, and let God take care of the situations that I am facing. Even though some of these challenges have brought great pain, I am really trying to come from a place of love rather than from self-ego. I can affirm that I know that to be true! I feel like I should be able to bench press an elephant by now, but can still see a whole herd of them coming. I pray that I am as strong as I need to be to weather whatever else may come. I am trying to sum the reading up, because I could keep going on and on, about how spot on Freddie was with everything he said to me.

Trey asked me to quit crying so much and to try and move forward and be happy. That he was proud of me and proud of what I am doing in his memory; telling his story. That I am going to do a lot of good with this and help a lot of people. But that I am also not sure of myself and I second guess myself. He said I need to believe in myself. That he and my other family members in spirit are backing me in this venture. As Freddie, put it, "giving me a push."

There is much more, but I feel like I am writing a book, so I will end it with this. At the end of the reading, Freddie told me that Trey was to my right side. Freddie asked me if I had a candle burning to my left; which in fact I did. He said that Trey was acknowledging the candle. But besides that, I could really feel my son at my side. I could feel the tingly sensation or chills or electricity all over my right side. This happens to me often and I can feel and sense his presence.

I can't thank Freddie enough for once again helping me in some much needed healing; his words of encouragement, that I needed to hear and knowing they were validated by some of my family in Heaven.

When the producers of "The Doctors" TV show reached out to me and asked if I would talk to them about my sons' story, I prayed and prayed and asked for a specific sign. If this was it, if this was what I was supposed to do, to send me a hummingbird. I had feeders out in my backyard but I hadn't seen any hummingbirds. In fact I was getting discouraged that they may not find me this year. I had been filling and replacing the feeders weekly and no sign of any hummers to my dismay. Well, the day came that it was time for me to decide and commit to doing the show or not.

I was on the phone speaking to one of the producers and was looking out my back door. To my surprise there was not just one, but four hummingbirds all over my backyard. I was on the phone and I was trying not to cry while I was speaking and finalizing a few details on how we would proceed. When I got off the phone, I went out into my backyard and a hummingbird flew right in front of my face and hovered for a good 15 or 20 seconds; close enough that I could feel the wind from his wings on my face. If I would have put my hand out, he could have landed on it. There are simply no words adequate enough to say how beautiful and magical that was. It was my SIGN and there could be no clearer validation than that it was on a bigger scale than I could have imagined. This happened twice more in the next two days while I was preparing for the interview. That is one of my *latest* visits from Heaven. To know that Spirit is backing me on this venture; cheering me on from the other side, and having Freddie validate that as well in my reading. Thank you again Freddie from the bottom of my heart ♥

Trina King

Update 1/27/2013

Hi Freddie,

How are you doing? I have been so busy moving. I haven't been on Facebook or the computer since early December.

276

A lot is going on in my life. I just wanted to let you know, when I was packing, I came across a very old tobacco pouch with a very old pipe in it. I remember my mom saying it was my grandfathers. So yes, he did smoke a pipe.

Funny how those things come back and re-validate our readings.

Love and light, Trina

What I am Up To Today

I still live in New York City and I will continue to live in this great city because my family is here and I don't want to leave them. I need their presence, support, and love in my life. As I am finishing this book, my 96-year-old mother, Mercedes, is with me – thank God. I am her primary caregiver and it is a job that I feel blessed to have been given. I would not trade this opportunity for the world.

By profession I have been a graphic artist, but I now choose to devote my time to helping those who need closure and healing by way of mediumship; it is my calling. The chapter "Proof Positive" is a testament to that.

In wrapping up my book; I want to express my deep appreciation to you for sticking with me through this long journey. My hope is that it has informed and enlightened you in many ways.

I hope that everyone will learn to feel compassion and understanding for children who may be experiencing life a little differently than their peers. I experienced ups and downs, confusion and fear about abilities that, as I learned later in my life, were, in fact, gifts from God. There are many of us out there who have endured these experiences alone. I hope painful experiences like mine will one day be a thing of the past.

I pray that this book touches your life and supports your freedom to live as your true self. I want to inspire and incorporate these gifts into all of our lives; it is more than attainable.

The natural tools and means of communication I have described for you have been used by diverse cultures throughout history. They have often been misunderstood or forgotten, even rejected, by many modern societies. Some religious dogma teaches that psychic abilities, our wonderful gifts from God, are instead the work of something sinister. I hope to reawaken our soul-deep knowledge of the primary purpose in being here on this earth plane. We need no longer fear any so-called "unknown" when we understand and embrace our true natures as spiritual beings having an earthly experience.

With God's help and that of my ascended brother Jesus Christ, as well as with the help of my angels and spirit guides, I will continue my work in mediumship. I have come a long way in my proficiency at delivering messages from loved ones in the afterlife. I have shared with you my growth and experience. I feel blessed by the great gifts I have received and the healing that has been achieved.

I live my life in such a way that if I take, I need to give back. I will continue doing volunteer work with organized bereavement groups.

My spirituality has transformed me into the person I am today, and if that weren't so, I feel that I would have been lost. Thank you, God!

Contacting Me:

My personal web site: http://www.mediumfreddierivera.com

GLOSSARY

This Glossary is provided courtesy of the Psychic Library (http://psychiclibrary.com). I thank them for being so generous in allowing me to use their definitions.

The following isn't a whole glossary of psychic terms, but only the ones that are used in this book. If you need further explanations, please do a search on your favorite Internet search engine.

Afterlife – The nonphysical world, which we occupy when we are no longer physically alive. "Eye-witness" accounts describing the afterlife from people who have had near-death (NDEs) are well documented.

Akashic Record – A universal filing system that is on a nonphysical plane of existence. It holds all human incarnations, events, feelings, thoughts, deeds and intentions for the past, present and future.

Apparition – An unexplainable, ghostlike image of a person or animal, or the appearance of something not of this world.

Astral Plane – It is part of the multi-dimensional series of planes surrounding us, which vibrates on a higher frequency than the physical plane. Angels, spirit guides and spirits transitioning to other planes reside here.

Astral Projection – Also known as astral travel; the experience of moving through different planes of existence and locations, in which the conscious self leaves the physical body.

Attachments – Also called spirit attachments, they are our past lives and experiences that we carry throughout life. They dictate the paths we choose. Attachments can be positive or negative. When possessed by negative attachments, they can be identified and sometimes removed through an Akashic record reading.

Aura – A band of colored energies surrounding every living thing that represents their life essence. It contains information about physical, emotional and spiritual health. Psychics, mediums and healers can see or sense the auras and are able to heal and cleanse unwanted energies within the body.

Chakra – Sanskrit term for "spinning wheel." Concept originated from Hindu medical practices and writings, which describe whirling, circular energy centers in the body that regulate physical and spiritual wellness. There are seven major chakras, each with a specific function: Root, Sacral, Solar Plexus, Heart, Brow (Third Eye) and Crown.

Channeler – One who communicates with the spirit world or facilitates healing through their higher self or spirit guides.

Channeling – To allow a spirit to communicate through the physical body or mind of a medium.

Clairalience – The ability to smell scents from the spirit world or from those who are not physically nearby.

Clairaudience – Also known as "clear hearing," the ability to hear words and sounds from the spirit world.

Claircognizance – Also known as "clear knowing," the

ability to psychically know something without being told.

Clairgustance – The ability to psychically perceive tastes without actually tasting anything.

Clairsentience – Which means clear sensing, is the ability to feel the present, past or future physical and emotional states of others, without the use of the normal five senses. Psychics who are clairsentient are able to retrieve information from houses, public buildings and outside areas. It is also one of the abilities used in aura sensing and psychometry.

Clairvoyance – The term clairvoyance, or clear seeing, originated from the French words clair (clear) and voir (to see). It is the ability to see events from the future, present and past within the mind's eye. Clairvoyance differs from telepathy, which is one of several other psychic powers. Telepathy is a conscious, direct sending of information from one individual to another, without the use of the five senses. Clairvoyance is the knowledge of past, present or future events that is gained without direct conscious thought.

Clairvoyance encompasses precognition — knowing events that are going to happen and retrocognition (postcognition) — knowing events or situations that have taken place in someone's past. In the field of parapsychology, clairvoyance falls under the category of psi-gamma. Clairvoyants use their ability to see or perceive events; whereas, some psychics and psychic mediums rely on angels and spirit guides or deceased individuals to obtain information.

Cold Reading – A technique used by pseudo-psychics to deceive people. The basic principle involves drawing out information from people without them realizing it is being done. It makes it seem as though the individuals have true psychic abilities, even though they do not.

Crossing Over – The point in time when a human or animal leaves the physical world and enters the spirit world.

Divination – The practice of predicting the future and discovering unknown facts by using tools, objects and supernatural means.

Earthbound Spirit – A deceased person's soul whose energy lingers in the physical world and has not yet crossed over into the spiritual realm. These spirits stay earthbound for various reasons.

Elementals – Energies of the earthly elements that take on various spirit forms from nature — earth, air, fire and water (for example, fairies). Used in Shamanism, occult practices, and by psychics to aid in their abilities.

Empath – A person who experiences and feels another person's emotions.

Energy – Positive or negative vibrations, which exude from the earth, people, spirits, or the universe as a whole.

Entity – An unexplainable energy that can take many forms but may or may not have an attachment to a human or animal spirit.

Fairy – A large variety of supernatural creatures that may be good or bad.

Free Will – The ability to choose a particular course of action when given multiple alternatives.

Ghosts – From the German "geist," or Old English "gast;" spirits of dead people who may be loved ones watching over us, tortured souls seeking justice for their untimely demise or murder, or those that do not realize they have crossed over to the other side. Often these spirits or specters do not recognize that we exist in the physical world because they are focused on their own plane of existence.

Grounding – To actively focus on one's physical connection to the earth. Useful for balancing when someone works within the psychic realm.

Haunting – An event that continually occurs where a ghost has taken up residence in the physical world.

Healer – Someone who uses medicine, herbs, energy, faith or psychic abilities to alleviate maladies within the body aura or chakras.

Human Aura – An oval, energetic field made up of levels that surround the body. It holds our current or former emotions, attachments, feelings and experiences. Each level contains its own vibration and can be translated into a color with its own meaning.

Intuition – The ability to know something without the use of logic or conscious reasoning. Knowledge gained by feeling, not fact.

Kabbalah – The Jewish book of mysticism taken from the Torah. It is the teaching of mystical activity and has been open to much interpretation because of its occult and metaphysical significance (see Metaphysics). Different spellings exist due to the fact that some letters in Hebrew have more than one usage in English.

Lucid Dreaming – The awareness that one is in a dream state while one is asleep.

Meditation – An internal, personal process that takes the mind into a heightened state of awareness in order to relax and heal the mind body and spirit.

Medium – A person who can communicate with humans or animals who have passed on to the other side and who has knowledge of the living who surround a person's life. These abilities can be present at birth or surface later in life through a traumatic experience or illness.

Mediumship – Communication with humans and animals who have passed to the spirit world.

Metaphysics – A branch of philosophy dealing with such abstract concepts as being, knowing, time and space.

Mind's Eye – To "see" with the mind; receiving visual mental imagery without actual visual stimuli.

Necromancy - Also known as nagomancy; a divination where conjuring or communicating with spirits are used to predict the future. Some practices involve the disinterment of a dead body.

Other Side – A dimension in which the spirits of people and animals who have passed reside; also known as the spirit world.

Out-of-Body Experience (OBE or OOBE) – A sensation of floating outside of one's own physical body or the perception of the body outside of itself.

Paranormal – Events or phenomena that cannot be scientifically explained.

Phenomenon – An event or incident that cannot be scientifically explained and whose cause is questionable.

Precognition – Knowledge of an event before it happens, in particular, a paranormal event.

Premonition – An intense feeling that something will occur in the near future.

Psi-Gamma – A category of study in parapsychology, which refers to the ability to acquire information through nonsensory or nonphysical methods, such as in telepathy, clairvoyance and precognition.

Psychic – An individual who has supernatural and varied abilities to sense things or access facts with little or no previous knowledge. Not all psychics are mediums, but all mediums are psychic.

Psychic Attack – The act of perceiving negative energy around you. This negative energy can be given intentionally or merely felt.

Psychometry – The ability to pick up impressions, visions, thoughts or events relating to someone just by holding an object, piece of jewelry, photograph or letter belonging to that person. It is also known as clairtangency or clear touching.

Reiki – An alternative healing therapy in which the practitioner channels and directs life-force energy through the palms of their hands to the meridian centers in the body.

Reincarnation – A soul's rebirth into a new physical body.

Residual Haunting – Repeated images or sounds of a ghost that previously resided in a place in the physical world, but is no longer actually there. No interaction takes place with the living.

Séance – A gathering, often lead by a psychic or medium, at which people try to contact spirits who have crossed over to the other side. A lighted séance is different from one held in the dark. At times, questions are first written down and the medium answers them with the alleged help of a spirit guide, the questioner's spirit guides or the departed loved ones.

Skepticism – A state in which the mind is closed off and doubts or questions things; sometimes this state can obscure the truth.

Smudge Stick – Originally used by Native American Shaman, it is a bundle of dry herbs (white sage is the most common) or other plants, leaves and incense sticks, tied together with string and burned. The scents from the burned smudge stick facilitate spiritual cleansing, clear negative energy or an entity, create harmony and are used in meditation and for medicinal purposes. An alternative to burning a smudge stick is the use of a scented spray, which is just as effective.

Specter – A term for ghost or spirit.

Spirit – The energy that continues on after an individual or animal has passed away. Spirits have the ability to appear as they were in life or in other forms, and they can communicate with the living through dreams and by transferring their emotions to and through us.

Spirit Guide – Entity from the other side, not necessarily a deceased relative, who is assigned to us at birth to guide us through life and keep us on a certain path. Usually from an ancient civilization, a spirit guide can appear as an animal totem, a Native American, Egyptian, Asian, Hindu, or have no specific ethnic attachment. Psychics and mediums generally refer to their guides by name and call on them when giving readings.

Spirit World – The realm in which the souls of humans and animals exist after crossing over from the physical world.

Spiritualism – A belief in the continuation of life and the existence of a spirit world. Its practice involves connecting with your higher self, which allows you to communicate or receive guidance from the heavens.

Spiritualist – A person who believes in spiritualism, has a deep respect for nature and all that is believed to come from the heavens.

Supernatural – Events, energies or personal powers that are unexplainable through the laws of nature or science.

Tarot – First known as "tarocchi" or "tarock;" a divination that uses a pictorial, 78-card deck to predict the future and interpret the past and present. In the English speaking world, the technique is considered a form of cartomancy. The numerology is usually thought to be significant. The Tarot is often considered to correspond to other divination systems such as astrology, Kabbalah, I-Ching and others.

Tarot Spread — The order in which tarot cards are laid out for a reading. There are many types, variations and number of cards used. Specific spreads are used for particular inquiries.

Telepathy – Also known as mental telepathy, the ability to transfer and receive thoughts and feelings from one mind to another. It is referred to as a sixth sense and is considered a form of extra-sensory perception (ESP). There is no formal training for this ability and it is not limited to psychics.

Third Eye – A concept referring to the brow chakra, located in the middle of the forehead and is associated with psychic abilities such as visions and clairvoyance. It is a psychic energy center.

22064836R00167

Printed in Great Britain
by Amazon